Public Relations and Individuality

Our individuality is partly shaped by encounters with the external world so it is inconceivable that we are unaffected by the planned management of public communications which manages much of our external experience. Exploring one of the most important mediators between organizations and individual encounters – public relations (PR) – is long overdue. By developing new ways to create and connect with us as members of particular target audiences, has it changed our interior existence by altering perceptions of the world outside ourselves?

PR's massive impact on groups, society or organizations is rightly explored, but its immense influence on our individuality is neglected. In an age where new media makes deepening connections to individuals, the relationship of PR to individuality is one of the field's most profoundly important issues. This provocative book will assist scholars and advanced students in PR and communication research to develop a clear, structured, disciplined understanding of this phenomenon and its implications.

Simon Moore is Senior Lecturer at Bentley College, USA where he specializes in public affairs, issues and risk management, crisis planning, developing new business proposals and environmental communication. He has published, presented and consulted in Britain, Canada and the United States and is the author of several books.

Routledge New Directions in Public Relations and Communication Research

Edited by Kevin Moloney

Current academic thinking about public relations (PR) and related communication is a lively, expanding marketplace of ideas and many scholars believe that it's time for its radical approach to be deepened. *Routledge New Directions in PR & Communication Research* is the forum of choice for this new thinking. Its key strength is its remit, publishing critical and challenging responses to continuities and fractures in contemporary PR thinking and practice, tracking its spread into new geographies and political economies. It questions its contested role in market-orientated, capitalist, liberal democracies around the world, and examines its invasion of all media spaces, old, new, and as yet unenvisaged. We actively invite new contributions and offer academics a welcoming place for the publication of their analyses of a universal, persuasive mind-set that lives comfortably in old and new media around the world.

Books in this series will be of interest to academics and researchers involved in these expanding fields of study, as well as students undertaking advanced studies in this area.

Strategic Silence
Public Relations and Indirect Communication
Roumen Dimitrov

Visual Public Relations
Strategic Communication Beyond Text
Simon Collister and Sarah Roberts-Bowman

Public Relations and Individuality
Fate, Influence and Autonomy
Simon Moore

Public Interest Communication
Critical Debates and Global Contexts
Jane Johnston and Magda Pieczka

For more information about the series, please visit www.routledge.com/
Routledge-New-Directions-in-Public-Relations–Communication-Research/
book-series/RNDPRCR

Public Relations and Individuality

Fate, Influence and Autonomy

Simon Moore

LONDON AND NEW YORK

First published 2018
by Routledge
2 Park Square, Milton Park, Abingdon, Oxon OX14 4RN

and by Routledge
52 Vanderbilt Avenue, New York, NY 10017

First issued in paperback 2020

Routledge is an imprint of the Taylor & Francis Group, an informa business

British Library Cataloguing-in-Publication Data
A catalogue record for this book is available from the British Library

Library of Congress Cataloging-in-Publication Data
A catalog record for this book has been requested

ISBN 13: 978-0-367-66677-4 (pbk)
ISBN 13: 978-1-138-29433-2 (hbk)

Typeset in Times New Roman
by Wearset Ltd, Boldon, Tyne and Wear

To Sandra

Contents

Acknowledgements

I would like to first thank my wife Dr. Sandra den Otter, whose scholarly scrutiny I continue to call in aid. I also want to acknowledge the friendship of, and insights obtained from (even if they may not have known it) Rob Brown, Lee Campbell, Ian Cross, Emile Flavin, Bernie Kavanagh, Rahul Kumar, Charles Marsh, Ruth MacSween, Sean McDonald, Graeme Mew, Mike Michelin, Salley Ouellette, Cliff Putney, Matt Sherar, Javed Siddiqi and Henri Weijo.

Next I want to recognize the advice and observations of Pierre Berthon, Jon Ericsson, Bill Gribbons, Roland Hübscher, Lynn Senne, Terry Skelton, Soterios Zoulas; and everyone else in the Information Design and Corporate Communication Department at Bentley University, Waltham, Massachusetts.

Bentley's excellent library service has been essential, along with Jasper, Simone and Lucas Richer, and my daughters Sophie, Imogen and Isobel. It is a boon that Sophie studies health and life sciences, and Imogen engineering mathematics. They helped me to glimpse more of the universe through my particular grain of sand; an objective of any writing, and also of parenthood.

David McKie, Tasos Theofilou, Tom Watson and Jordi Xifra are responsible for two collegial and thought-provoking conferences: the annual International History of Public Relations Conference at Bournemouth in the UK and the annual Barcelona International Critical PR Conference. I doubt this book would have been written without the stimulus these events have provided.

Finally and always: Kevin Moloney, Editor of the Routledge New Directions in Public Relations and Communication Research series. His inspiration for the series has helped elevate PR's place in scholarship by setting out the remarkable extent of its impact on society. This is my second book for the series, which means I am once more fortunate enough to thank everyone at Routledge for their usual efficiency and kindness, including Jacqueline Curthoys and Laura Hussey, along with Emma Critchley, Claire Bradley and Meridith Murray.

1 PR and individuality

The book is about the connections of public relations (PR) to individuality, and how those connections are changing. Individuality in this book is the measure of the individual's autonomy and consciousness, which changes because of PR. Philosophical, scientific and technical considerations appear only as they seem useful to understanding what PR does to and with the individual.

If we want to understand individuality, let alone the workings of the world, PR matters for several reasons. It is a practical activity used by every kind of organization; widespread enough to warrant the same academic attention as, say, accounting, finance, marketing or management. On another level PR goes further because, borrowing from the title of one of the first books on the subject, it is what societies use to engineer consent on a big scale and not always successfully. PR can be a creative force in its own right, applying imagination to deliver experiences to chosen publics, sometimes by operating in near-equal partnership with them, sometimes by pretending to. PR frequently determines the subjects we discuss, the aspects of them we talk about, the tone we use to discuss them, and offers perspectives that affect views on other subjects as well.

PR is a business but was never just a business activity, if defined by what it actually does instead of what it might be called at any particular time in history. Its methods long predate the needs of business, and it is used by many types of organizations and people. PR is present in almost every area of human activity: in warfare and parenthood, selling and voting, image and reputation, corporations and communities, policy-making and the generation of emotion. PR's enormous range and the media it can use make it of interest to the arts and sciences. It is an arbiter of our senses in an era of closely managed information and as such it is an arbiter of power and a power in its own right.

Since PR's business is with humanity it must know what makes humanity tick. It is an unrecorded presence in several academic disciplines. We need not look hard to locate PR in, among other subjects, communication studies and semiotics, and in history, politics, psychology, philosophy and technology. It may attract little attention from students of these fields but there it is anyway. The ubiquity is essential. PR must make use of those subjects and many others to manage relationships between organizations and people, which ultimately means between organizations and individuals. To be of any use PR's varied activities must converge on that one point – that is, on each one of us.

And when that happens what happens to us? The question is as yet unanswered. After all, PR usually scales its resources to reach people in volume. As one among many, an individual must feel reaffirmed as part of a group: a small audience or a big public that seems to matter for personal, social, civic or commercial reasons, if only for a short time. Yet whenever something is presented through the prism of a group, it is done to move individuals in a particular direction. The aggregate effect on individuality must be at least as significant is it is for larger groups. How has PR changed individuality and how will individuality change PR?

Our individuality is the first and last vessel of instincts, reason and experience, both the 'I' and the 'you' with whom we all must have relations. PR's connection to it is immense and insufficiently understood. To this observer at least, it seems to be profound and historic. Profound because of the huge period of time in which activities now grouped under the title of PR have been at work, gradually intensifying and diversifying to take in larger numbers of individuals with larger numbers of messages that, for good or not, encourage or provoke particular behaviours. Historic because in that time PR reconfigured individuality itself by affecting personal and collective decisions. It is evidence for what has been called 'the reality-making power of public relations within the context of historical time, culture and place' (St John III, Opdycke Lamme & L'Etang, 2014, p. 2).

Individuality evolves if PR is active. That claim can be made because our choices are not separate from our individuality. Choices are not programmed responses to managed messages aimed at our many public identities. They are the result of changes to the way we individually and inwardly choose to see ourselves. Changing individuality itself might be a scarcely noticed by-product of a PR campaign, but it may be PR's most enduring impact.

The book is partly explained by saying what it is not. Its first, not-chosen title was 'Public Relations and the fate of the individual' which I still like for its philosophic, impressionistic and even mythological undertones. For practical reasons the publisher suggested 'Public relations and individuality', I think rightly. The interconnections between PR, philosophy and certainly mythology are many and varied, but in the end 'fate' should be less prominent. It is a little too mystic to bear the burden of the task assigned to it. Its underlying reference is to that which has been predetermined, which cannot be avoided, and it is too often used if the predetermined end is unhappy. There is no historical and still less mystical inevitability about the *detail* (or unhappiness) of PR's effect on our individuality, although possibly its *general* impact on individuality was irresistible for reasons developed in these pages.

This is not a book about mass or any other kind of media, except when they serve PR. The independent influence of newspapers, television, the internet and other media on society has been much studied. Setting state propaganda aside for now (it appears later), less attention has been paid to the impact on our individuality of planned, carefully targeted communication applying customary and unexpected media and messages, and all the other paraphernalia needed for strategic perception-shaping. Nor is this a book about any noise purely associated with *selling*. PR and its antecedents work for products, organizations or people in the realm of ideas, of perceptions, and of the feelings suggested through them. Its usually unspoken purpose is to build connections in a more lasting and far deeper way than, say, pushing an immediate purchasing decision. Therein lies one source of its authority.

This is not a polemic. I do not say that PR's impact on individuality is only bad. PR works at too many levels, and in too many ways, for such a judgement. It may in fact signal that individuality is respected by society. When a definitive moral judgement seems necessary, though, it is offered.

As an aside and in connection with making a judgement, PR's need to promote public actions with public media is one more reason to read (and write) books. Marshall McLuhan wrote in 1964, 'The book form is not a communal mosaic or corporate image but a private voice' (McLuhan & George, 2013, Chapter 21). Writers have the fortune and opportunity of expressing ideas through an unalloyed medium for individuality. PR is sometimes too inclined to reward groupthink.

It is hoped this book is not the last word on its chosen subject. If we are to protect, project and know our 'self', we must know more about PR and individuality. The chapters in this book are linked essays, hopefully introductions to bigger inquiries. An initial attempt must be made because the subject is very urgent.

This *is* a book about the related and parallel expansion of planned PR activities and individuality's changing nature. PR is the newest name for a very old practice. It is often pointed out that many activities gathered under the name 'public relations' originated many thousands of years ago: started in fact when our emerging consciousness as individuals led people to organize and cooperatively preserve a collective identity as members of a group. The next chapter makes a case that parts of the process began even earlier than that. These first steps towards organized group communication could have been prompted by competition from rival groups, and the compromises individuality was ready to make for sustenance and reproduction advantages conferred by group membership. Communication for the organization grew more complex, more competitive, more essential, and needed more resources, planning and more power hierarchies. Soon a point was reached whereby organizations reversed the hierarchy of communication itself. Their leaders took over the controls and required cohesion from individuals, who at most became a lesser collaborator in the communication process. This transfer of organized public communication power from loosely individuals to largely organization came quite late to humans. It was a momentous development for managed public communication and human individuality.

We must field walk several subjects to find the connections between individuality and group communication, and the effects of PR's unceasing attempts to alter, weaken or strengthen individuality to achieve momentary purposes. Humans have journeyed across time in company with carefully managed public communication by organizations. That ancient and usually un-named task (which for convenience I shall mainly call by its present day name of PR, or 'managed public communication' wherever 'PR' seems distractingly contemporary) and its impact on individuality can be understood by means of philosophy, science, history, psychology, social studies, the work of businesses, governments and other organizations and of course PR research. This book is written in the hope that isolating specialisms do not multiply and cut off access to studying PR's place in them. Thankfully, PR scholars avoid this since, to repeat an earlier remark, their business is with humanity itself.

A comment by the scientist and philosopher Jacob Bronowski could also be adjusted to PR's manifold invocations:

> The idea that one can conjure the world with names, with nouns, and even with verbs is a familiar belief among primitive peoples.
>
> (Bronowski, 1978, p. 44)

It is not valueless to think about PR's conjurings from the standpoint of individual belief in them. PR is not just a function. Its immateriality and individual desire for what it promises make it akin to an alternative belief system. In fact, PR's future with individuality is a pressing matter for society. Biological media for contacting audiences and most of all individuals are coming. Some early examples are described starting in Chapter 4 but newer machines will take their place before this book goes to print. Let us collectively call them 'biomedia'.

Biomedia alone means PR must know much, much more about individual human biology, but proceed with care if possible. It has been said about Marketing:

> Neuroscience offers new ways to measure heterogeneity in consumer behavior by measuring differences in individual sensitivity across regions or structural differences in the brain.
>
> (Camerer & Yoon, 2015, p. 424)

We mustn't claim too much for neuroscience, for now at least, and especially not to the exclusion of other disciplines. Borrowing from *Hitchhiker's Guide to the Galaxy*, neuroscience is not Life, the Universe and Everything. It might occasionally be looking in the wrong places. There are 'serious challenges posed in trying to examine the biological processes underlying or associated with social psychological phenomena' (Harmon-Jones & Devine, 2003, p. 589). Subjective elements in PR and possibly human biology should alert us to C. G. Jung's caution that in scientific inquiry: 'Every answer of nature is therefore more or less influenced by the kind of question asked, and the result is always a hybrid product' which 'misses out on all those by no means unimportant aspects that cannot be grasped statistically' (Jung & Hull, 2011, Chapter 1).

Not that PR can ignore Science. It is systemizing old knowledge PR uses instinctively, and classifying new findings in highly suggestive ways. Science helps us glimpse what PR is doing to individuality, including its biology. Some research supports the idea that humans communicate competitively to achieve neurological, evolutionary advantages. Communication itself evolves with the advantages that are achieved, creating a higher form communication like PR: higher because it strategically manages public communication between humans in organizations and other groups, applying complex technology as extensions of our principal organs of communication. The new technology of biomedia and the messages it carries could soon participate in reconfiguring the human body. Cognitive science is investigated as well in later chapters. It is a neglected theoretical and practical link between PR and neuroscience.

Advances in the disciplines just mentioned, and others, have enormous strategic, creative and ethical consequences for PR. Will individuals still need to belong in groups, groups that PR finds useful to contact and invent? Is there a point to reaching them if group-directed media is obsolete or ineffective? Are we on the verge of more open, transparent and incredibly creative kinds of PR? A new age for media, messages and manipulators?

The British psychologist and cyberneticist F. H. George (1921–97) deserves to be better known for his thoughts on artificial intelligence (AI) and communication, and through them to PR. In *Philosophical Foundations of Cybernetics* he observed:

> We can achieve a kind of certainty only about our own feelings and impressions and these are, to the extent that they are certain, private and uncommunicable, or at least difficult to communicate. The observer is certainly imprisoned to some extent in (certainly limited by) his own private world and can only derive so much from his contact with reality.
>
> (George, 1979, p. 81)

In spite of this, the observer is also the target audience for organizations, and frequently desires to admit an organization's interpretation of 'reality' into this private world of feelings and impressions. Why is this so? PR is a key to that desire and it is about to take up technology of unprecedented power.

It is time for PR to understand individuality in more detail. There is much to learn at the place where neuroscience, communication, AI and the individual connect, and 'society' is set aside. If a more individual-centred era of PR is coming, science may offer society at least some insights into what PR does with, for and to the individual. We must ask about the ways that human biology, which includes the nervous system, explain our invention of PR as well as its many works. The final answer might well be that our nervous system sheds little light on PR. At the moment there are good reasons for thinking otherwise. At this moment the search for questions and answers must begin.

Future PR may be able to merge the objectives of an organization with the nervous system and psychology at a deep level, deeply diffusing into the ways people feel and reason. Would PR of that sort drop communication and take up pharmacology? This book traces the steady conversion of the human individual into a PR device: into media, message and audience, and perhaps soon, a PR 'patient'. Finally (for the moment), individuality seems set to leave humans behind altogether, and PR will change once again.

These are subjects all must think about. To build on a recent book in the Routledge series (Brown, 2014) *The Public Relations of Everything* includes the PR of us. The persuasive part PR plays is not unlike that played by History, which was described 200 years ago by the philosopher G. W. F. Hegel as the act of 'transferring what were previously mere extraneous happenings into the realm of intellectual representation' (Hegel & Nisbet, 2010, First draft). To get organizations to objectives, PR does with the past, present and future what historians do with the past. PR is everywhere in time and space, unfixed from a single principle, but it is a system of representing knowledge to justify a human need intellectually and by concrete actions.

What follows then is an attempt to understand PR's impact on each 'everyone' it wants to engage. There is no doubt that PR works with and on constituent elements of individuality, but unlike other human activities it can appear to offer few insights or little content of its own when it is at work. Its activities vary historically but at a given moment are often derivative and repetitive. It makes no proclamations and claims of its own. It is premeditated and planned, and made to achieve somebody else's purpose, usually without the targeted public knowing much about how it happened. Insubstantiality, joined to managing an organization in the public sphere, give PR its peculiar power. Initially it serves those it represents. Eventually the position is reversed and rival organizations, products, people, societies competing for advantage must to some degree adjust to PR's remorseless demands, changing their words, actions, identities however reluctantly to meet the realities of managed public communication. Competing PR activities are 'invisibly' forging new assumptions about perception, about society, and as will now be seen, about individuality.

The terms 'conscious' and 'unconscious' appear in these pages. They are described in more detail later but it is helpful to briefly – very briefly – reference the ways they are mainly interpreted in the book. 'Consciousness' broadly means 'subjective experience' (Barrett, 2014, p. 1): our awareness of our own selfhood and the exterior world we encounter; the 'unconscious' describes the latent symbols, myths, underlying and often dormant experiences and other archetypes that guide much of our response to the exterior world.

The book's structure should be described. The next two chapters (2 and 3) look for fundamental, universal, elements binding individuality to PR. It may be true that 'the person or self has been studied in only a small fraction of human societies' (Spiro, 1993, p. 107), but there appear to be traits common to all human individuality. Some of them explain our need for PR. Those elements which combined into what today is called PR were at work in the early stages of human evolution, making the rudiments of PR into a fundamental individual desire.

The next four chapters (4 to 7) largely ask how the evolution in managed public communication changed individuality, and the last two chapters ask how individuality and PR are about to be extended beyond the control of human beings.

PR and individuality have changed each other. No more can be done here than marking some of the broadest forks in the road of change, but they matter. Kant explained in *The Critique of Pure Reason* (1781) that objects are representations, and the pure form of what they represent cannot be known: our perception and knowledge are limited. This may be correct, but there is an intensely human desire to get at the pure form of things. Satisfying that desire is one reason PR exists. It is right then to reflect on what PR has done to individuality, is doing now, and seems likely to do in the future.

References

Barrett, A. B. (2014). An integration of integrated information theory with fundamental physics. *Frontiers in Psychology*, 5, 63. Retrieved from http://journal.frontiersin.org/article/10.3389/fpsyg.2014.00063/full.

Bronowski, J. (1978). *The origins of knowledge and imagination*. New Haven, CT: Yale University Press.

Brown, R. E. (2014). *The public relations of everything: The ancient, modern and post-modern dramatic history of an idea*. Abingdon, Oxon: Routledge.

Camerer, C., & Yoon, C. (2015). Introduction to the journal of marketing research special issue on neuroscience and marketing. *Journal of Marketing Research (JMR)*, *52*(4), 423–426.

George, F. H. (1979). *Philosophical foundations of cybernetics*. Tunbridge Wells: Abacus Press.

Harmon-Jones, E., & Devine, P. G. (2003). Introduction to the special section on social neuroscience: promise and caveats. *Journal of Personality and Social Psychology*, *85*(4), 589.

Hegel, G. W. F., & Nisbet, H. B. (2010). *Lectures on the philosophy of world history: Introduction: reason in history*. Cambridge, UK: Cambridge University Press.

Jung, C. G., & Hull, R. F. C. (2011). *Synchronicity: An acausal connecting principle*. eBook. Princeton, NJ: Princeton University Press.

Kant, I. (1965). *Critique of pure reason*. New York: St. Martin's Press.

McLuhan, M., & Gordon, W. T. (2013). *Understanding media: The extensions of man*. ebook. New York: Gingko Press.

Spiro, M. E. (1993). Is the Western conception of the self 'peculiar' within the context of the world cultures? *Ethos*, *21*(2), 107–153.

St. John III, B., Opdycke Lamme, M., & L'Etang, J. (2014). Introduction: Realizing new pathways to public relations history. In B. St. John III, M. Opdycke Lamme & J. L'Etang (Eds.). *Pathways to public relations: Histories of practice and profession* (pp. 1–8). Abingdon, Oxon: Routledge.

2 PR and individuality

'Roots and beginnings'[1]

Problems

PR could not exist without the individual. PR knows this but has said surprisingly little about it. Practice and scholarship in the field often bypass the individual (except for some important ones), and concentrate on groups. This does not alter the fact that the individual must form relations with groups on a spectrum running between enthusiastic, uncertain and reluctant.

PR's path must take it into the minds of individuals. The routes may vary with the place, polity and time and occasionally PR finds that the individual is not always inclined to give ground to the organization. Custom or law roughly regulates the balance between the two. In some societies people are officially encouraged to develop as individuals largely through their own ideas and initiatives, which help define the extent of their contacts with other people and organizations. Some states try to build special protections for this idea of the individual against its idea of a group, whether the group is a loose association of other individuals gathered for recreational or charitable purposes, or the representatives of a business, or of the state. Meanwhile, other states or powerful organizations mandate closer conformity to an interest, product, institution, ideology or government in the hope of achieving particular commercial, political, behavioural or religious goals. All societies tinker with the degree of individual cooperation or subordination to group needs. The life of individuals is often spent negotiating these relationships, weaving into identities of differing sizes and resources: families, employers, corporations, states and so on. Wilfred Trotter, a pioneering neurosurgeon and social psychologist, noted in 1915:

> It is obvious that when free communication is possible by speech, the expressed approval or disapproval of the herd will acquire the qualities of identity or dissociation from the herd respectively.
>
> (Trotter, 1919, p. 40)

It seems important to understand the part PR plays in this and if that makes PR a problem for individuality. This book tries to identify which elements of individuality are most affected by PR, and to assess those effects in detail.

The general effect is surely considerable. PR delivers impressions of exterior experience to our interior experience, and on a colossal scale measured by time or volume of information. Ephemeral or enduring, the cumulative impact of PR's activities on our individuality cannot be ignored by anyone who feels with John Donne that 'I am involved in mankind'. This is so whatever the extent of our involvement. PR's methods cannot be ignored by anyone agreeing with the libertarian Robert LeFevre that the best way to constructive involvement with humanity is 'self-ownership' (LeFevre, 1966/2007, Chapter IV). Or at the other pole, ignored by those who accept Marx, Engels and Lenin's arguments of an economic struggle between individuals gathered into enormous 'classes', for whom they defined and publicized separate political identities. Or ignored by dictators believing with Marx or Lenin, campaign groups and corporations that desirable results would come from subsuming sufficient of our individuality into an appropriate mass. To lesser or greater degrees this intense, dynamic and often revolutionary process of immersing individuals (and in some cases vainly attempting to dissolve them entirely) in bigger audiences remains the main route taken by PR on behalf of brands, causes, sports, public figures, governments, non-profits or products over and above the challenge of recognizing individual 'self-ownership' standing above audiences.

If there are problems divining the connections between PR and individuality, the first are logistical and historical. The task is large and the areas open to exploration larger still. We stand before a vast mass of time, technology, material prosperity, human nature, the competing claims of organizations or things, seamed with a near-infinitude of managed communication experiences. The events of the last 200 years alone have complicated the task. The creation of publics where individuality experiences dilution if not dissolution is not unique to an urban, industrial, age. Still, it was certainly invigorated and enlarged by industrial and urban growth, which developed well-managed public communication managed in ever-closer detail. When Gustave Le Bon wrote in 1895: 'The divine right of the masses is about to replace the divine right of kings' (Le Bon, 2001, p. xi) he was in accord with other acute observers of nineteenth century society, including Karl Marx, Thomas Carlyle, Edgar Allen Poe, Charles Mackay and J. S. Mill. Le Bon also knew the masses desired direction, whether they knew it or not, and that it was a task for communication. Others drew the same conclusion. 'There can be no talk', wrote Lenin, 'of an independent ideology being developed by the masses of the workers in the process of their movement'. 'Our task' he continued, 'the task of Social-Democracy, is to *combat spontaneity* [original italics]' (Lenin & Christman, 1987, p. 82). Hitler wrote more reverently of the life of the individual (if they were Germanic), until it came to his own designs for them, at which point his prescriptions resembled Lenin's:

> The function of propaganda does not lie in the scientific training of the individual, but in calling the masses' attention to certain facts, processes, necessities, etc., whose significance is thus for the first time placed within their field of vision.
>
> (Hitler, Manheim & Rogers, 1971, p. 179)

These trends from individual to group are by no means only modern or political, although PR is inseparable from politics. If the word 'revolution' means anything at all we can say that in the nineteenth century, a revolution in media, communication, information management and perception started that continues to accelerate and leave behind the industrial revolution that started it. New media stimulated the individual's senses, and organizations learned how to apply it. Those best-known from the industrial age down to our time – including mass-produced newspapers, electronic media, the internet and social media – are potent enough. They can exploit less publicized developments that invigorated information. The creation of synthetic dyes from petroleum by-products and minerals in the nineteenth century, to take one example, enlarged the palette for the human eye and created vivid new options for organizations. Such innovations appeal to the senses. They succeed because they engage individual perception, our constituent biology and perhaps other components of our personality. PR's power and potential is strengthened by such ostensibly indirect developments, but their often profound contributions are harder to see and assess.

Second, how to retrieve our individuality – or at least those features of it within reach of PR – from the same aggregate of time, people and tools? Psychology, history, philosophy and biology cluster around this enigmatic subject, far more mysterious to us than our understanding of the group, and producing more variable opinions. The problem cannot be overlooked. Anyone studying individuality should know something of PR. A helpful start is to ask why and how our individuality emerged and which aspects of it were most open to the activities that became PR. For that reason the balance of this chapter reflects on PR's connections to fundamental elements of our individual identity as they developed from deepest time, namely: consciousness of our individual nature, the connections between our consciousness and symbols or signs, and between our individual self and other individual selves.

Beginnings

Emergent individuality and emergent PR

We must talk about the individual if we take PR seriously, but we must extrapolate many possibilities from limited facts, and begin at the beginning. Ideas about individuality's origins are notably tentative, but we must talk about individuality based on what evidence there is of its beginnings. What we find is helpful for understanding PR's authority in society and over people.

It is at least a fact that human experience is locked into the dimension or as many philosophers and physicists propose, the illusion, of time. We shall see later how PR shapes individuality by frequently adjusting perceptions of past, present and future, coaxing us towards a helpful version of temporal progress. PR's variable use of time has made a profound impact on our individuality, but taking the most familiar strictly linear perspective, starting in the deep past and moving forward towards our position in time, it is likely that the need for organized communication to influence a group preceded the emergence of highly-evolved individuality. A tremendous expansion of consciousness of our individuality is shown by the painted images and symbols of the Upper Palaeolithic 40,000 years ago, marking a process that has intensified up to the present.

Yet this evidence of a creative consciousness is the vivid fruit of older processes, processes that helped start the long-drawn out evolution of the several human species, and probably existed before that. There is group communication in many other animal species, including the higher primates, and we can make connections between that more limited communication and personalities in a band, herd or pride. This earliest period did though eventually generate complexity and plasticity in specifically human group communication, evidenced by the time and energy spent on more creative and sophisticated uses of media: the treatment of minerals or bones to make paints, associating particular rock surfaces with the forms of particular animals, choosing specific locations within caves for symbols and images. The group learned how to use communication practically and imaginatively in increasingly sophisticated and dynamic group situations.

Before humans there was an older fundamental need, or desire, to shape or manage perceptions of other individual organisms, in a limited way. We will later ask how PR appears to satisfy traits that originated in the time before human species, let alone before the appearance of human individuals realized enough to be described as 'the measure of all things', the phrase used by the pre-Socratic Greek philosopher Protagoras (c.490–420 BC) (Plato, 'Theaetetus', 1997, 152a).

Little writing survives from Protagoras, but his observation epitomizes another practical link between self-realization, perception, knowledge and the communication of knowledge. It appears in Plato's *Theaetetus*, written c.369 BC. *Theaetetus* was a discussion about the nature of knowledge between Socrates, Theodorus the mathematician and a young man, Theaetetus. The first and biggest of the three definitions of knowledge offered by Theaetetus is that 'knowledge is simply perception' (Plato, 'Theaetetus', 1997, 151e) which Socrates encapsulates using Protagoras' celebrated words, before picking Theaetetus' definitions apart. In the end they cannot reach a single definition. Instead, led by Socrates, the trio inconclusively discuss several ideas about knowledge: whether it is the elements of a thing that is to be understood, or personal perception, or the element that distinguishes a piece of knowledge from other things, and whether the balance between individual or communal understanding is a factor. Not even Socrates can help the group reach a definitive understanding of knowledge and that failure, perhaps, illustrates humanity's rarely satisfied search for conclusive knowledge, for perceptions that are true, or at least believable, and therefore for agents to deliver them persuasively. During that delivery the individual naturally responds to the techniques that were used, and so the idea of knowledge may grow more subjective than objective, while the quest for definitive answers continues. Since Plato at least, PR and its antecedents have prospered because of 'the assumption that any serious question must be capable of a correct answer' (Berlin, 1973, p. 4).

In the civic and commercial sphere conditions are set for a lasting and unresolved relationship between the individual and the management of public communication for organizations. Protagoras and Socrates are raising one of the earliest conditions for connecting individuality to what in time became PR: a continuous need for information, generating authentic or even conclusive knowledge. An eternal hope for resolution means PR can wrap itself into a desiring individual consciousness.

For any group looking to organize, this individual consciousness was naturally necessary for communication. Receptiveness to symbols or signs was the second condition. The third was the ability to infuse symbols and signs with myths expressing key information about the group. One result was an individual open to group messages and willing to surrender parts of individuality in exchange for the benefits of being in an organized community. Another was the rise of people who achieved organization by managing symbols. These conditions should be examined in more detail.

Consciousness: arbiter of communicated experience

Consciousness of our individuality is surely the starting point for managed public communication. Consciousness is a sufficiently immense field in its own right, and in the words of a clinical investigator: 'persists as a fundamental question in science and philosophy' (Mashour, 2012, p. 19876). It seems more likely to exist than not, but awaits a universal concrete definition, if such a thing is useful or possible. When viewed narrowly as a PR necessity, consciousness is closely related to contact with physical and conceptual stimuli, prompting perceptions and actions from blends of the imagined and the material. For this book, the word 'consciousness' is the consciousness of our 'self' that expresses, receives and processes our desire for increasing knowledge, and weighs relations between group and individual, including power relations. There is value in René Descartes' proposal in *Principia Philosophiae* (1644) that thought must at times process the material world, the 'realm of extension' in which our body's materiality connects with other material things. Freud took up this theme in *Civilization and Its Discontents* (1930) when he wrote: 'With all his tools man improves upon his own organs, both motor and sensory' (Freud & McLintock, 2004, Chapter 3). The gramophone record and camera 'are essentially materializations of his innate faculty of recall, of his memory' (Freud et al., 2004, Chapter 3).

As far as PR is concerned consciousness, or something very like, is a crucible where individual and group relations are frequently recast, creating a balance of communication between the two negotiated in the 'realm of extension'. The academic and remarkable media seer Marshall McLuhan (1911–80) appears to have read Descartes and Freud. McLuhan's famous assertion 'the medium is the message' captures this restless relationship between group and individual in *Understanding Media* (1964), thanks to media which he called 'extensions of man' in the book's subtitle:

The personal and social consequences of any medium – that is, of any extension of ourselves – result from the new scale that is introduced into our affairs by each extension of ourselves, or by any new technology.

(McLuhan & Gordon, 2013, 'In a culture')

Harnessing the media that shapes or extends individual consciousness into society is a condition for PR's influence. It encourages what may be called a dynamic consciousness, far more active, comprehensive, complex and self-directed among humans than any other single species. This ability to 'extend' is connected to our biology. Descartes thought of mind and body as essentially different things. Contemporary research suggests interconnections between the two produce an awareness that opens individuals to larger communication possibilities. The scientist and philosopher Jacob Bronowski proposed that from the first evolved, large-brained humans, individuality benefited from highly developed physical senses to encounter the world, to imagine and create. In the 1967–68 Silliman lectures published as *The Origins of Knowledge and the Imagination* (1978) Bronowski presented two sequences to characterize the path to these aspects of consciousness: ' "visual," "vision," and "visionary"; "image," "imagery," "imagination" ' (Bronowski, 1978, p. 18). Bronowski laid particular stress on sight and language. He proposed that understanding individuality as creative, autonomous, reflective, culture-creating, active, depended on studying the biological origins of those and other communication capabilities: 'the modes of perception, of speech, and of symbolization' (Bronowski, 1978, p. 6). The psychologist C. R. Badcock enlarged on these views when he described the dynamic element in consciousness as 'a plasticity of behaviour and an elaboration of activity' (Badcock, 1983, p. 2). These, he and others have suggested, were stimulated by the avenues for reflection opened by particular physical traits including an opposed thumb and forefinger, the greater importance to reasoning of sight over scent, the ability to stand on two legs, an enlarged cerebral cortex able to undertake complex tasks, and complex language skills.

The hypotheses just described give insight into two other just-mentioned conditions PR needs from the individual. The first is symbolic thinking and therefore receptivity to symbols. The second is a higher order of ability to identify and collaborate with groups. The communication dynamism unlocked by these two conditions was intensified by a third: ordered rather than anarchic competition within and between groups.

Perhaps it is relevant to PR that Badcock, echoing Freud, connects this last condition of intricate rules-based competition to the overthrow of the first group leader or father by his younger male relatives. According to Freud the outcome of this was the discovery 'that the group could be stronger than the individual' (Freud et al., 2004, Chapter 4), with the result that 'restrictions' had to be imposed 'to sustain this new state of affairs' (Freud et al., 2004, Chapter 4). The idea of an ordered group identity regulated and motivated by management of sometimes competing signs and symbols may originate in these earliest networks made by media, messages, imagination and human desire to use symbols to the point where: 'one thinks in symbols – that is what thought is' (Berlin, 1965, p. 10). In those circumstances consciousness and communications are not separate points in a hierarchy, but interdependent and changing in relationship to each other. PR participates in a continuous, shifting, as yet unresolved dialogue between the two connected to the unsatisfied personal desire for conclusive knowledge described earlier.

The debt consciousness owes to competition, and so to communication from competitors, could be connected to another competitive struggle in the womb. This is because of the possibility of 'genetic imprinting' or the 'silencing' of one set of parental genes by genes from the other parent, as opposed to equal expression. Some research indicates rivalry between 'brain-expressed' genomic imprinting from either the father or the mother (the genome is the complete set of DNA, including genes, required for an organism) (Davies et al., 2008, p. 62). Experiments with mice suggested that those injected with two maternal and no paternal genomes 'displayed relatively large brain: body size ratios' and those injected with genomes in reverse proportion displayed the reverse result (Davies et al., 2008, p. 64). Badcock described the consequences for diploid organisms (organisms with two sets of chromosomes each donated by a parent), raising themes familiar to a student of PR activity:

> Conflict between thought and feeling, instinct and intelligence, emotion and cognition, appears to be written into the genetic code, built into the brain long before birth and played out in life forever afterwards.
>
> (Badcock, 2004, p. 219)

Nor can consciousness be understood without understanding the mind. In *Neurophilosophy*, Professor of Philosophy Patricia Smith Churchland argues that 'mental processes are brain processes':

> It is most unlikely that we can devise an adequate theory of the mind–brain without knowing in great detail about the structure and organization of nervous systems.
>
> (Churchland, 1986, p. 482)

Experiments have suggested that the elements of consciousness do not disintegrate when the human subject is placed under certain anaesthetics, although the functions that synthesize the elements of consciousness into a more unified experience are suppressed:

> Primary sensory networks are maintained during anesthetic-induced unconsciousness, whereas multimodal association areas and internetwork connectivity appear differentially susceptible to the effects of anesthetic agents.
>
> (Mashour, 2012, p. 19876)

Science's fusion of mind and body does not augur well for PR claims about promoting dialogue, let alone creative persuasion. Is PR really throwing biological switches to direct our nervous system and warring strands of DNA? Does it really come into play because individual consciousness autonomously seeks to resolve or express biological instincts for communication, competition and conflict in the exterior world beyond the self? If this is so, PR has historically thrown switches that control spiritual or non-rational content. It seems PR must somehow graft that content onto the facts of human biology. It must offer experiences that 'explain' or 'unify' a host of smaller experiences or sensations, draw a 'fragmenting consciousness' (Mashour, 2012, p. 19876) into a whole that satisfies the individual experiencing it.

There is then evidence indicating that, if nothing else, individual consciousness is quite deeply embedded and tough. Apparently it takes a great deal to disrupt or destroy it: the death of the individual, or a modified and chemically-assisted imitation. It might be inferred that this gives considerable authority to any activity or thing that can connect with an individual's 'multimodal association area' to synthesize sensory experience into a clarifying consciousness. Still more authority would be conferred on a function that can to some extent provide synthesis on the area's behalf by coordinating information and impressions delivered to the apparently unsleeping 'primary sensory networks'. On these bases it may have been inevitable that PR, whose evolution alongside human consciousness is explored here, has always experienced a growing and now extremely strong influence over key elements of consciousness that compose our individuality.

That influence appears to depend on the individual's desire to reconcile biology to things that are not biological, and are sometimes not scientific, and are often without physical reality outside the mind, unless there is a non-material reality beyond the mind but accessible by it. In communication this particular desire is satisfied by symbols, and their role as tools to manage perception, famously studied by the neurologist and founder of professional psychoanalysis Sigmund Freud (1856–1939). Freud sought to understand his patients through their dreams by 'transforming the content':

> Either by replacing it piecemeal in accordance with a fixed key, or by replacing the dream as a whole by another whole to which it stands in a symbolic relation.
>
> (Freud, Strachey & Gay, 1989, p. 7)

Freud ended the just-quoted paragraph in *On Dreams* (1900) with a wry comment about a problem with his approach which PR shares: 'Serious-minded people smile at these efforts. *Träume sind Schäume* – "dreams are froth"' (Freud et al., 1989, p. 7). It was to establish PR as something considerably more than froth that Freud's American nephew Edward Bernays (1891–1995) wrote a series of pioneering books on the subject from the 1920s onward, and built a considerably successful career as one of the first professional PR practitioners. PR was more securely established by 1985 when one of Sigmund Freud's great-grandchildren, Matthew Freud, launched his highly successful PR business in London.

In their different roles both the Freuds and Edward Bernays assert the value of engaging the individual consciousness in a convincing interaction by using symbols to synthesize impressions. *Träume sind Schäume* to those unable to look past the surface of tasks that compose a busy exterior life, but not so to others who can read symbols, and their power to encapsulate meaning, and their impact on individual consciousness.

Consciousness and PR: symbols, signs, myths

An immense subject now presents itself, the use of symbols converting the individual need to communicate into a way to communicate with groups or as a group. Symbolic thinking is essential to individual identity and expression. Scholars of semiotics have examined the effects on thought and language, of symbols, signs, the myths they often came to express, and their various uses from earliest times. PR's use of these assets has attracted less attention than it has for advertising, politics and religions, perhaps because those functions historically use highly obvious symbols in highly visible media. Nevertheless, when it comes to symbols the three last-named functions are parts, in the case of advertising a rather small part, in a more extensive and overlooked PR-like superstructure of symbol coordination. The 'invisible government' of PR notably described in 1928 by Edward Bernays (Bernays & Miller, 2005, p. 37) uses signs and symbols more flexibly, pervasively and for many purposes. 'Public relations practitioners' it has been pointed out, 'can be called symbolmakers if one considers their work is largely word and image' (Mickey, 1997, p. 271). In 1955 Doris Fleischman and Howard Cutler proposed: 'A symbol, in the sense it is used in public relations is representative of a theme'. The theme is the campaign's 'story line' or central concept (Fleischman & Cutler, 1955, p. 138). Understanding PR's influence on individual consciousness requires understanding why the individual responds to the way PR uses symbols to serve themes.

Signs and symbols are terms often used interchangeably. There can be no definitive distinction for them inside PR – how could it be otherwise for such a fluid activity? It would be at best short-lived to agree on one. Occasionally however they are defined differently. A sign might show itself in an event or ritual, as well as in a material thing, an appeal to one or all of the senses. 'Sign' *and* 'symbol' are used to describe something that occupies less time and space than events or rituals: a single visual artefact, for example, or a short spoken sequence within a larger event. Both are applied in PR because they can stand for something outside of the immediate present or the observable order, to depict an ideal, appealing to what Jung called the 'collective unconscious' of the group. They express values that have become embedded in a culture by means of a myth, and often feel essential to the individual's attachment to that culture. Anthropologists Alcorta and Sosis offer a helpful distinction between 'symbols' and 'signals' (not signs): 'Signals are necessarily bound to the moment; symbols, however, have existence and meaning that extend beyond the immediate to link the past, present, and future' (Alcorta & Sosis, 2005, p. 350).

How can symbols manage this? Jung simply said: 'we constantly use symbolic terms to represent concepts that we cannot define or fully comprehend' (Jung, 1968, p. 4). Liberated from concrete restrictions and directed at the imagination, vague concepts can have strong communication power. In their study of religious ritual Alcorta and Sosis recognize its communication and neurological qualities:

> The symbolic systems of religious ritual in early human populations solved an ecological problem by fostering cooperation and extending the communication and coordination of social relations across time and space.
>
> (Alcorta et al., 2005, p. 325)

This does not fully explain why symbols in particular possess such qualities. Alcorta and Sosis concur with researchers who *inter alia* link religious symbols with the release of stimulants like dopamine, 'a neuromodulator which functions as a reward for the organism' (Alcorta et al., 2005, p. 333), notably in adolescence. Froese, Woodward and Ikegami studying origins of symbolic material culture, cautiously suggest an approach which combines 'empirical data of neuroscience and verbal descriptions of first-person experience in a mutually informing and enriching manner' (Froese et al., 2013, p. 208). While Froese et al. accommodate the subjective experience of individuals, an unanswered problem is to explain the evolution of the particular solution of dopamine-triggering 'species-specific signals' (Alcorta et al., 2005, p. 344) alongside the development of a 'symbolic mind' (Froese et al., 2013, p. 200). The Platonic answer might be that all things are the physical expression of an ideal 'being or essence' (Plato, 'Cratylus', 1997, 423e), signs of 'something that is not the Form but has its character whenever it exists' (Plato, 'Phaedo', 1997, 103e).

In all such interpretations 'essence' in communicated symbols appears beyond the reach of purely rational, empirical investigations. Nevertheless it is at least widely agreed that signs and symbols stimulate imagination while individuals act inside a group. This ability for symbols to mediate in the hierarchies that groups inevitably generate may be another reason for their appeal to individual consciousness. Symbols and signs, as Alcorta and Sosis imply, help groups manage their identity, the lives of their members, and conserve energy and resources. Another use of symbols was to help modulate displays of aggression and non-aggression within the group and with rival groups. The opinion of French reactionary philosopher Joseph de Maistre (1753–1821) was shared across the political and philosophical spectrum when he wrote that 'the legislator cannot gain obedience by force or by reasoning' (de Maistre, 1994, p. 57). Force and reason are never enough to sustain a group. The qualities unlocked by the symbol also mattered.

By supporting codification or custom, symbols and signs can constrain individuality and justify the dominance of some individuals over others. Freud commented:

Perhaps one may begin by declaring that the element of civilization is present as soon as the first attempt is made to regulate these social relations. If no such attempt were made, they would be subject to the arbitrary will of the individual; that is to say, whoever was physically stronger would dictate them in accordance with his interests and instinctual impulses.

(Freud et al., 2004, Chapter 3)

For these reasons a main purpose, perhaps the first purpose, of signs and symbols in PR is an often non-rational appeal to deep feeling, arousing what the philosopher, psychologist and physician William James called 'the reality of the unseen' (James, 1994, p. 61) in *The Varieties of Religious Experience* (1902). It is an evocation to bring individual imagination into alignment with a desired outcome: commercial or political, mundane or inspirational. Bernays believed the job of PR was 'organizing chaos', the first chapter title of his account of the subject in *Propaganda*, published in 1928 (Bernays et al., 2005). Organizing chaos by signs and symbols takes Sigmund Freud's work with his patients, enlarges the scale, and interprets a symbol as the soul of a particular organization, product, idea or person. Thomas Mickey is among those who recorded ambiguous consequences: 'Public relations practitioners manipulate the image because they know the importance people place on signs and symbols in our culture more than on truth' (Mickey, 1997, p. 279). This passage is not suggesting PR invariably lies. It is saying that postmodern interpretations are right to suggest symbols are frequently more important to people than the Truth, that PR is fully aware of this, and that the individual must therefore be exposed to symbols in public communication managed by organizations.

It is inevitable from this that signs and symbols are assets to be contested and owned. Like knowledge itself, they were objects of inquiry by the ancient Greeks. Semiotics itself originated from debates in Athens over natural signs and signs deliberately designed for communication (Cobley, Jansz & Appignanesi, 2010, p. 5). The Epicurean philosopher Philodemus of Gadara (*c.*110–30 BC) reports differences between Epicurean and Stoic thinkers about the origins of 'signs' and how they are interpreted by the individual, and if they are understood universally or according to individual inference.

The Epicureans hold that the sign is perceived, while the Stoics hold that the sign is intelligible, and grasped only by thought.

(Philodemus, 1941, p. 174)

If symbols, individual consciousness and PR are to operate together for any reason, there must be competing alternatives. Whether the meaning of symbols is instinctively grasped, or interpreted by human reason, there must be rival meanings to be corrected that are either dormant or actively communicated. This being the case a premium is clearly placed on the best ways for achieving success. Success is 'conversion through symbolization', a phrase used in a medical context by Sigmund Freud and the physician Joseph Breuer in 1895 (Breuer, Freud & Strachey, 2013, Chapter II, Observation V).

A symbol in the public domain seeks conversion from its audiences. To do this it may be attached to the non-rational, usually by expressing an archetypal myth that legitimizes an organization in the individual imagination. It was an enormous step in managed public communication that assisted solidarity and the territoriality needed for early group survival. An organization's culture could henceforth be justified by a mythology. It was a step that depended on other emergent individual characteristics. These were foresight and imagination, and the capacity to anticipate or create information needs suggested by sophisticated sensory perceptions. Sensory development of the sort described earlier by Bronowski, Badcock and others had opened more avenues for non-instinctive, non-reactive, forms of reflection and shaping opinion. Symbol-making became a compelling way of engaging individuals on more and more subjects. Signs and images could be arranged to extend beyond their literal meanings, and send abstract, time-transcending messages. Myth-signs and myth-symbols enriched the procedure and brought the believing individual closer to a shared group imagination.

Under these conditions the relations between symbols, managed public communication, media technology, individuality and society could grow more interdependent, more sophisticated and more costly. The resources used to manage the process possibly contributed to failures of early states and cultures that the original activity was meant to uphold. In *The Collapse of Complex Societies* (1988) anthropologist and historian Joseph Tainter discusses the destabilization created by rising costs and diminishing returns of expensive and complex 'sociopolitical control and specialization' (Tainter, 1988, p. 115) and 'information processing' (Tainter, 1988, p. 99) by a hierarchy that must 'bond a population to itself' (Tainter, 1988, p. 117).

Symbols as myth-communication: Cassirer and Jung

In the twentieth century, the features Tainter described became yet more costly, complex, intense and confrontational, to the appalling point of confirming his theory. Two prominent figures studying the consequences of social turmoil for individuality were the philosopher Ernst Cassirer and the psychologist Carl Gustav Jung. Their work was affected by witnessing (and in Cassirer's case, escaping) dictatorships in Europe, warfare, and societal collapse. Both men treated symbols, myth and consciousness as hard historical, psychological, evolutionary and political realities. In this way they demonstrated what individuality owed to managed public communication, and the continuing desire to connect with material and non-material worlds beyond the self.

Ernst Cassirer (1874–1945) was a German exile from Nazism who died in New York City shortly before the end of the Second World War. His experience of totalitarianism spurred him to reflect on the state's ability to reach into the individual, and subvert his autonomy. His last books, *An Essay on Man* (1944),

Language and Myth (1925) and *The Myth of the State* (posthumously published in 1946) are valuable for anyone interested in what PR may be doing to the individual, and why it can do it. Cassirer did not confine himself to one academic discipline, and consequently his work had a wider impact. A passage from *The Myth of the State* was read in Spandau Prison by Albert Speer, once Hitler's Architect and Armaments Minister. It presents the problem that Speer, other individuals, and PR itself, must resolve:

> But here are men, men of education and intelligence, honest and upright men who suddenly give up the highest human privilege. They have ceased to be free and personal agents.
>
> (Cassirer, 2013, p. 286)

Cassirer's explanation, like Jung's, was the state's subversion of a spiritual realm by managed public communication. It worked because the connection between symbols, myth and individuals was ancient and innate: 'the immediate *perception of the Infinite* has from the very beginning formed an ingredient and a necessary complement to all finite knowledge' (Cassirer, 2013, p. 20). The active agents were symbols, encapsulating language and myth to channel individual autonomy. In totalitarian states alternative interpretations of regime-backed symbols were forbidden.

Cassirer rejected ideas of myths as simple daubs of primitive societies, treated as literal because of an incapacity to grasp metaphor or simile. That was to misread myth as a pathological problem, in which it is 'explained as a mere disease' (Cassirer, 2013, p. 22). Myth is not that:

> It is closely connected with all other human activities – it is inseparable from language, poetry, art and from early historical thought. Even science had to pass through a mythical age before it could reach its logical age: alchemy preceded chemistry, astrology preceded astronomy.
>
> (Cassirer, 2013, p. 22)

Language is also part of myth, but not the reason for it. In an important passage Cassirer wrote: 'It is not a very satisfactory and plausible hypothesis to think of human culture as the product of a mere illusion – as a juggling with words and a childish play with names' (Cassirer, 2013, p. 22). In the words of the translator of Cassirer's *Language and Myth*, Cassirer's insight was 'that *language*, man's prime instrument of reason, reflects his mythmaking tendency more than his rationalizing tendency' (Langer in Cassirer, 1953, Preface). In Cassirer's words:

> Myth has, as it were, a double face. On the one hand it shows us a conceptual, on the other hand a perceptual structure. It is not a mere mass of unorganized or confused ideas; it depends upon a definite mode of perception.
>
> (Cassirer, 1992, p. 76)

The potency of symbols and myth are visible signs that PR is more or less a phenomenological model: a structured activity integral to some biological elements of consciousness, steering it towards objectives. Neurologist, psychiatrist and concentration camp survivor Victor Frankl argued in 1955 that the ultimate objective was not material, 'that something like a striving for moral status exists' which 'longs' 'for an immortalizing of the self in some durable form' (Frankl, 1986, Part 1). Successful symbols and myth make a PR activity intrinsic to the receiver, converting a material need into a non-material state that the individual actually desires. In these conditions the power to manage myth-making signs and symbols, including ritual symbols, becomes more important than the content. In Cassirer's words: 'it is only by symbols that distinctions are not merely made, but fixed in consciousness' (Cassirer, 1953, Chapter 3). Cassirer recognized their power to convey a state of feeling outside reasoned intelligence, as posited by the prominent French psychologist Théodule-Armand Ribot. McLuhan's famous insight that the media is the message is also supported by this potent characteristic of signs and symbols. They were after all present at the earliest encounters between medium, message, organizations and individual, which were predominantly formally religious or informally superstitious.

McLuhan's insight is foreshadowed by Cassirer, for example in the last sentence of this comment on religious rituals:

> When performing a religious ritual for ceremony man is not in a mere speculative or contemplative mood. He is not engrossed in a calm analysis of natural phenomena. He lives a life of emotions, not of thoughts. It has become clear that rite is a deeper and much more perdurable element in man's religious life than myth.
>
> (Cassirer, 2013, p. 24)

Drained of religious credence, but not of their ritual authority, established symbols are adapted to serve more political ends. This appears in Plato's *Republic* when Socrates makes the famous and very practical suggestion of a 'noble falsehood' to bind people to the Republic by the use of magic, music and ritual (Plato, 'Republic', 1997, 414b). One outcome of politically exploiting the individual's spiritual capacity were the totalitarian states of Cassirer's troubled time, channelling Hegel, who as quoted by Cassirer wished the state to represent the ' "Divine Idea as it exists on earth" ' (Cassirer, 2013, p. 263).

Individuality, the state and symbols were also a concern of C. G. Jung (1875–1961). I have written of Jung elsewhere but he cannot be overlooked here (Moore, 2014, pp. 118–128). Aside from a PR agency in Stockholm that may be named after him (a nice parallel with Freud's relatives), Jung's connection to PR – like Cassirer's – is via reflections on state propaganda. They rest on theories Jung first developed with Freud and later independently as he developed the idea, noted earlier, of a 'collective unconscious' open to many influences. In brief Jung's work with his patients led him to believe that the human mind consisted of conscious contact with the busy material world; the personal unconscious of often repressed but still extant life experiences including traumas; and the collective unconscious, which Jung explained as:

> An unconscious psychic activity present in all human beings which not only gives rise to symbolical pictures today, but was the source of all similar products of the past.
>
> (Jung, 1933, Chapter 3)

The symbolical pictures of the collective unconscious 'spring from – and satisfy – a natural need' (Jung, 1933, Chapter 3). A symbol seeks to represent spiritualized, possibly dormant, content in the unconscious. It appears to be a factor in the individual's never-completed search for true information already discussed in the chapter, and in Jungian terms helps or hinders the path to individuation: 'the urge toward unique, creative self-realization' (Franz in Jung & Franz, 1968, p. 167). To Jung, a symbol 'implies something vague, unknown, or hidden from us' (Jung & Franz, 1968, p. 3). His interest in propaganda rose from the archetypes politicized symbols generated in the collective unconscious, drained of authentic spiritual values by modern states, and communicated to societies swept up in the conscious material world and vulnerable to deceiving versions of the collective unconscious.

Jung shared Cassirer's concerns for individuality. In *Memories, Dreams, Reflections* (1961) he warned:

> To live and experience symbols presupposes a vital participation on the part of the believer, and only too often this is lacking in people today.
>
> (Jung & Jaffei, 1989, Chapter IV)

The needs of individual consciousness are displaced as an organization – in this case society organized through a state – grows in complexity. The individual is isolated. In *The Undiscovered Self* (1957), Jung argued that the individual's exposure to advertising and to 'communal propaganda' (Jung, 1990, p. 516), left him or her 'de-individualized' (Jung, 1990, p. 535), 'morally and spiritually inferior in the mass' (Jung, 1990, p. 536), and in 'an infantile dream-state' (Jung, 1990, p. 538).

Jung's nineteenth century predecessor on this subject was the prominent essayist Thomas Carlyle. Carlyle regularly expressed outrage at the corruption of symbols by the money and commerce of industrialism. He proposed new heroes to return society to virtue by re-invigorating symbols with new forms of faith and submission (Carlyle, 1829; 1839; 1843; 1887; 1908). Jung preferred to reawaken individual consciousness. It was fragile because it had submitted to symbols controlled by great men and states. Yet individuality was not extinguished because symbols:

> Have been ingrained in him from earliest times, and, eternally living, outlasting all generations, still make up the groundwork of the human psyche.
>
> (Jung, 1933, Chapter 5)

In the twentieth century individuals should repossess the symbols comman-deered by the state and 'remould those archetypal forms into ideas which are equal to the challenge of the present' (Jung, 1990, p. 548).

Plato's Socrates foresaw the advantages of participating in deceitful symbols, distinguishing between 'true falsehood' and 'falsehood in words'. The former was 'ignorance in the soul of someone who has been told a falsehood'; the latter was 'a kind of imitation', less offensive and even useful to the gods. Socrates asked: 'By making a falsehood as much like the truth as we can, don't we also make it useful?' (Plato, 'Republic', 1997, 382). A trait that could be useful to the gods might be useful to sustaining the perfect state. Jung on the other hand dep-recated the damage to individual consciousness when falsehoods were success-fully communicated by imperfect states. Even in democratic nations political propaganda 'may cause us to live in ways unsuited to our natures', causing a 'psychic imbalance' (Jung & Franz, 1968, p. 35). In other regimes worse damage was done to consciousness. 'Fanatical political activity', a leading Jungian psychologist wrote, 'seems somehow incompatible with individuation [the individual's journey toward distinctiveness]' (Franz in Jung & Franz, 1968, pp. 241–242). Jung went further in *Symbols of Transformation* (1956):

> Mass psychology is egoism raised to an inconceivable power, for its goal is immanent and not transcendent.
>
> (Jung, Read, Fordham & Adler, 1970, p. 104)

Jung and Cassirer matter to our subject. They show why PR seeks to 'own' symbols that are ancient, but not extinct and embedded in our individuality. Jung and Cassirer are among those who looked to human prehistory and to the essence of individuality, and made a direct connection between them and modernity. That connection was the process of communication reaching deep into con-sciousness by joining collective and mythologizing symbols to powerful media on an industrial scale. Given the times they lived in, their interest in myths and symbols organized by the state was natural, although they could be organized by other kinds of organizations. Bernays, working at the same time as Jung and Cassirer, understood this and a chapter on the subject appears in *The Engineering of Consent* (1955), which he edited. It was one among many insights he con-tinues to offer PR.

PR's roots are in the individual

We have already seen that the profound connections between individual con-sciousness and communicated experience are complemented and not dismissed by neurological research, including non-material content of organized communi-cation like religious rituals. Neurologists Saver and Rabin do not doubt that 'Religious experience is brain-based, like all human experience' and open to sci-entific inquiry (Saver & Rabin, 1997, p. 498). In 1995 the neurobiologist Jean Delacour recorded 'a clear tendency to consider consciousness as a scientific object' and argued that 'consistent subjective and objective explanations of con-sciousness are possible' (Delacour, 1995, p. 1061). It has also been proposed that 'many of Jung's reported perceptions sound like modern recountings now asso-ciated with the right temporal lobe' (Barnum, 2006, p. 351), with the result that his work 'has turned out to be the phenomena amenable to "hard science" empir-ical research' (Barnum, 2006, p. 357). At the very least, Jung and Cassirer provide a persuasive starting point for considering our individuality and the roots of PR's connection with it.

In these circumstances PR could not have originated inside organizations. Much more had to exist before that. Neither PR nor individuality can be under-stood, or be at their most effective, without considering the first contacts between human and consciousness through managed communication. These brought together artefacts, rituals, desires and organizations. Eventually goods today regarded as consumer goods were included in this 'spiritualizing' nexus, but that powerful source of PR activity came later. Few if any goods made at the dawn of human history and consciousness needed self-identifying organizations to brand them, though eventually they too turned into symbols, took on the values of organizations and played their gigantic part in PR's activities with the individual.

What does this account say about PR and individuality? It says PR is as old and tough as consciousness. It suggests modern PR and its progenitors are intrin-sic to our biology. It suggests that PR is integral to individual consciousness and cannot be wished away. It suggests PR's power is desirable for cognitive, neuro-logical reasons and that it seems undeniable that something else emerges from this connection, involving beliefs in a non-material reality, creative impulses and a wish for forms of clarification not obviously present in the world of material things. If nothing else, it suggests PR's future was decided at the earliest phase of human development. This chapter explored the 'roots and beginnings' of that lift-off, the necessary conditions for everything that has happened since.

Note

1 See *The Lord of the Rings: Fellowship of the Ring*, where the phrase is used to describe Gollum (Chapter 2).

References

Alcorta, C. S., & Sosis, R. (2005). Ritual, emotion, and sacred symbols. *Human Nature*, *16*(4), 323–359.
Badcock, C. R. (1983). *Madness and modernity: A study in social psychoanalysis.* Oxford: Blackwell.
Badcock, C. R. (2004). Emotion versus reason as a genetic conflict. In D. Evans and P. Cruse (Eds.) *Emotion, evolution, and rationality.* Oxford: Oxford University Press, pp. 207–222.
Barnum, B. S. (2006). Why Freud and Jung can't speak: A neurological proposal. *Journal of Religion and Health*, *45*(3), 346–358.

Berlin, I. (1965). Two enemies of the Enlightenment. 2. The First Onslaught: J. G. Hamann and his Disciples. Woodbridge Lectures, Columbia University, NY: 25–28 October. Retrieved from http://berlin.wolf.ox.ac.uk/lists/nachlass/hamann.pdf.

Berlin, I. (1973). The origins of cultural history. 1. Two Notions of the History of Culture: The German versus the French Tradition. Gauss Seminars, Princeton University, NJ: 19–22 February. Retrieved from http://berlin.wolf.ox.ac.uk/lists/nachlass/origins1.pdf.

Bernays, E. L., & Miller, M. C. (2005). *Propaganda*. Brooklyn, NY: Ig Pub.

Breuer, J., Freud, S., & Strachey, J. (2013). *Studies in hysteria*. (A. A. Brill, Trans.). Retrieved from www.digireads.com.

Bronowski, J. (1978). *The origins of knowledge and imagination*. New Haven, CT: Yale University Press.

Carlyle, T. (1829). Signs of the Times. In T. Carlyle, *Critical and miscellaneous essays*. Volumes 1–2 (1894 Ed.) (Volume 2, pp. 230–252). London: Chapman and Hall.

Carlyle, T. (1839). Chartism. In T. Carlyle, *Critical and miscellaneous essays*. Volumes 6–7 (1894 Ed.) (Volume 6, pp. 109–186). London: Chapman and Hall.

Carlyle, T. (1843). *Past and present*. Boston: Little, Brown.

Carlyle, T. (1887). *Reminiscences*. London: Macmillan & Co.

Carlyle, T. (1908). *Sartor Resartus. On heroes, hero-worship and the heroic in history*. London: J.M. Dent & Co.

Cassirer, E. (1953). *Language and myth*. (S. K. Langer, Trans.). eBook. New York: Dover Publications.

Cassirer, E. (1992). *An essay on man: An introduction to a philosophy of human culture*. New Haven, CT: Yale University Press.

Cassirer, E. (2013). *The myth of the state*. New Haven, CT: Yale University Press.

Churchland, P. S. (1986). *Neurophilosophy: Toward a unified science of the mind–brain*. Cambridge, MA: MIT Press.

Cobley, P., Jansz, L., & Appignanesi, R. (2010). *Introducing semiotics*. London: Icon.

Davies, W., Isles, A. R., Humby, T., & Wilkinson, L. S. (2008). What are imprinted genes doing in the brain? In: Wilkins, J. F. (Ed.) *Genomic imprinting*. New York: Springer Science & Business Media, pp. 62–70.

Delacour, J. (1995). An introduction to the biology of consciousness. *Neuropsychologia*, *33*(9), 1061–1074.

Fleischman, D. E., & Cutler, H. W. (1955). Themes and symbols. In E. L. Bernays (Ed.) *The Engineering of Consent. [Essays, by various authors.]*: Norman, OK: University of Oklahoma Press.

Frankl, V. E. (1986). *The doctor and the soul: From psychotherapy to logotherapy*. eBook. New York: Vintage Books.

Freud, S., Strachey, J., & Gay, P. (1989). *On dreams*. New York: Norton.

Freud, S., & McLintock, D. (2004). *Civilization and its discontents*. eBook. London: Penguin.

Froese, T., Woodward, A., & Ikegami, T. (2013). Turing instabilities in biology, culture, and consciousness? On the enactive origins of symbolic material culture. *Adaptive Behavior*, *21*(3), 199–214. Retrieved from www.researchgate.net/profile/Takashi_Ikegami/publication/258123821_Turing_instabilities_in_biology_culture_and_consciousness_On_the_enactive_origins_of_symbolic_material_culture/links/54dff85a0cf2953c22b47a3e.pdf.

Hitler, A., Manheim, R., & Rogers, D. (1971). *Mein Kampf*. Boston: Houghton Mifflin.

James, W. (1994). *The varieties of religious experience: A study in human nature*. New York: Modern Library.

Jung, C. G. (1933). *Modern man in search of a soul*. eBook. New York: Harcourt, Brace & World. North American eBook 2011, Christopher Prince.

Jung, C. G., & Franz, M. L. (1968). *Man and his symbols*. New York: Dell Pub.

Jung, C. G., Read, H., Fordham, M., & Adler, G. (1970). *The collected works of C. G. Jung: Symbols of transformation: an analysis of the prelude to a case of schizophrenia*. Princeton. NJ: Princeton University Press.

Jung, C. G., & Jaffeì, A. (1989). *Memories, dreams, reflections*. eBook. New York: Vintage Books.

Jung, C. G. (1990). *The undiscovered self: with symbols and the interpretation of dreams*. Princeton, NJ: Princeton University Press.

Le Bon, G. (2001). *The crowd: A study of the popular mind*. Mineola, NY: Dover Publications.

LeFevre, R. (1966/2007). *The philosophy of ownership*. eBook. Auburn, AL: Ludwig von Mises Institute.

Lenin, V. I., & Christman, H. M. (1987). *Essential works of Lenin: 'What is to be done?' and other writings*. New York: Dover Publications.

de Maistre, J. M. (1994). *Considerations on France*. Cambridge: Cambridge University Press.

Mashour, G. (2012). Fragmenting consciousness. *Proceedings of the National Academy of Sciences of the United States of America, 109*(49), 19876–19877. Retrieved from www.jstor.org/stable/41830428.

McLuhan, M., & Gordon, W. T. (2013). *Understanding media: The extensions of man*. New York: Gingko Press.

Mickey, T. J. (1997). A postmodern view of public relations: Sign and reality. *Public Relations Review, 23*(3), 271–284.

Moore, S. (2014). *Public relations and the history of ideas*. Abingdon, Oxon: Routledge.

Philodemus. In L. P. De & L. E. A. De (1941). *Philodemus: On methods of inference: A study in ancient empiricism*. Philadelphia, PA: American Philological Association. Retrieved from https://archive.org/stream/philodemusonmeth00phil.

Plato. (1997). 'Phaedo.' (G. M. A. Grube, Trans.). In J. M. Cooper and D. S. Hutchinson (Eds.) *Complete Works*. Indianapolis, IN: Hackett Publishing Company, 49–100.

Plato. (1997). 'Cratylus.' (C. D. C. Reeve, Trans.). In J. M. Cooper and D. S. Hutchinson (Eds.) *Complete Works*. Indianapolis, IN: Hackett Publishing Company, 101–156.

Plato. (1997). 'Theaetetus.' (M. J. Levett, rev. Myles Burnyeat, Trans.). In J. M. Cooper and D. S. Hutchinson (Eds.) *Complete Works*. Indianapolis, IN: Hackett Publishing Company, 157–234.

Plato. (1997). 'Republic.' (M. J. Levett, rev. Myles Burnyeat, Trans.). In J. M. Cooper and D. S. Hutchinson (Eds.) *Complete Works*. Indianapolis, IN: Hackett Publishing Company, 971–1223.

Saver, J. L., & Rabin, J. (1997). The neural substrates of religious experience. *The Journal of Neuropsychiatry and Clinical Neurosciences, 9*(3), 498–510.

Tainter, J. A. (1988). *The collapse of complex societies*. Cambridge: Cambridge University Press.

Trotter, W. (1919). *Instincts of the herd in peace and war. (Second edition.)*. London: T.F. Unwin.

3   PR, and the inner and exterior lives of individuals

Why does the inner life of the individual matter to PR?

Amid pressing deadlines, ceaseless public chatter and perpetual news cycles the idea that PR has any useful connection with individual consciousness looks obscure at best, irrelevant at worst. How can knowing individuality – as opposed to society – make PR more effective? What can individuality tell us about the society PR is affecting? Does it matter that an 'invisible' inner life of individuals is affected when the desires of a 'real' (visible) external world are publicized?

It helps to briefly reiterate why PR must exist. It exists as a function because the individual biologically and culturally wants it, not because organizations force it on them. Chapter 2 suggested PR's foundations were laid genetically, neurally and psychologically to which were added philosophy, history, technology, religion and politics as humans formed groups, of growing complexity.

PR's first significant, most recognizable, application – which continues to the present – was to keep the group together. One original reason – survival – was severely practical; another – a need for belonging – was not. The methods used might be described today as 'spiritually proto-political' and for a long time did not change much. For this reason it is unhelpful at this point to divide state from other communicating organizations like businesses, by making distinctions between propaganda and PR. When individuals seek the external world's material or conceptual assets, groups eventually form and cooperate in a formal system of governance, production and consumption. In all three last-named categories the fundamentals of public communication were almost identical to start with, eventually differentiating. The approaches were summarized in Chapter 2: engaging individual consciousness with myth-symbols from our unconscious which serve the purposes of a group; closer control over myth-symbols by organizations with a complex hierarchy; using them imaginatively to satisfy the individual's neural, creative, rational and non-rational needs; claiming a portion of the individual's beliefs and activities for the group; trying to present information that satisfies the urge for the truth behind whatever subject is being communicated.

That could only be done by managed communication between group and individual. That process, at first the preserve of religion and polities, eventually spread into commerce. Organizations then as now saw the value of influencing the individual's interior life by consistently communicating collective interpretations of myth and fact, on behalf of an organization's needs as defined by its leadership. A communicating authority balances the individual's interior experience with exterior experience. Chapter 2 described why the individual felt such intrusions were desirable, or inevitable, and was often willing to collaborate with it. This balancing activity is at the heart of PR: relations between organizations and publics must be planned and cannot be trusted to luck. What may have started capriciously and ad hoc must be sustained by building and managing a strategy, which puts increasing demands on organizations whose requirements grow more complex. Complex organizations ensured that individuality encountered them on more forms of media, and developed more reasons to intervene in individual consciousness. Early manifestations of this planned activity included closer attention to controlling the calendar, imaginative approaches to the organization of spaces and times, ownership of special landscapes and words or images, the involvement of a larger number of participants, new rules for balancing facts with feelings, and different kinds of organizations. Planned public communication was applied imagination, as useful in its own way as the hand axe or plough. With it the organization extended itself into the individual, and the individual into the organization. The inner and outer worlds of sense and experience could be mediated strategically and in detail.

The interior, inner life of the individual contributes to individuation; our existence as a distinct, aware, object in time and space, which was suggested in Chapter 2. There could be no PR without that inner autonomy. Lacking autonomy, individuals would merely receive not interpret exterior data, become vessels of collective not solitary activities, and cells in a groupthink directed by mechanics or chemistry. Engaging the individual's opinions or desires would be pointless. PR therefore is society's recognition that individuality is in fact configured very differently, is capable of personal autonomy, resists pure rationality and can for now often evade automated direction, even when a member of a target audience and even when searching for truth.

Where does PR connect with this interior experience?

PR and interior experience: points of contact

Obstacles

The question is hard to answer. One reason is that to a large extent PR remains Bernays' 'invisible government' (Bernays et al., 2005, Chapter 1). Law, medicine or engineering have their own public architecture, rituals, clothing, smells, noises and technologies. PR does not, and maybe cannot in the same way. It has no material public identity. It is everywhere and nowhere. It can only be expressed from the mind to the mind, using media common to society and not through an identifiably physical artefact called 'Public Relations'. PR might recognize itself in the lines of Lao Tzu: 'The whole world says that my way is vast and resembles nothing. It is because it is vast that it resembles nothing' (Lao Tzu, 2012, LXVII.163). It is almost incredible that so little attention has been paid to the implications of PR's non-materiality, which contains all of its value to organizations. The invisible aspects of individuality affected and used by PR have drawn limited attention. If something cannot be touched, smelled, heard, tasted or seen, the view seems to be, it cannot be spoken of because it does not physically exist and must be 'passed over in silence',[1] or only inferred without getting to grips with the subject.

The search for scientifically verifiable information is moreover hampered by 'the use of introspective techniques that may be less experimentally tractable' (Andrews-Hanna, 2012, a large-scale brain system) when studying 'intrinsic' features of the brain. These features include 'ongoing neural and metabolic activity which may or may not be directly associated with subjects' performance' (Raichle, 2015, 1. Introduction) but which use up a large proportion of the brain's energy – very little brain energy is consumed by actual task performance (Raichle, 2015, 2. Adjudicating the merits of intrinsic activity). A telling analogy has been made with the 'dark energy' of the universe (Zhang & Raichle, 2010). The available experiments compare unfavourably with those available to task-oriented areas of the brain amenable to 'extrinsic' systems like sensory and attentional functions (Andrews-Hanna, 2012, a large-scale brain system). The problem is an old one. Freud was sufficiently discouraged by it to separate psychoanalytic psychology from brain science, though he anticipated future reconciliation (Kandel, 2012, Chapter 5). Today, and despite the shortcomings, the weight of history, psychology, faith and lately neuroscience raise new possibilities for understanding PR's connection to the individual brain. Another valuable resource is cognitive psychology. Its founding father Ulric Neisser described cognition as 'all processes by which a sensory stimulus is transformed, reduced, elaborated, stored, recovered and used' (Neisser, 1967, p. 4). Neisser continued: 'Our knowledge of the world *must* be somehow developed from the stimulus input' (Neisser, 1967, p. 5). Such rich sources demand that an attempt must also be made to chart PR's stimulus input into the individual mind. It is part of PR's story and individuality's story: better knowledge of it encourages PR is to grow as an organizational function, scholarly discipline and change-agent.

Memory and PR

Memory is itself a medium for messages and perceptions. To influence society PR must intervene in the individual's memory, for 'our very sense of continuity and identity would be meaningless in the absence of memory, tied to the unfolding of our lives in time and their directedness to the future' (Teske, 2001, pp. 668–699). Memory has attracted considerable study. Theories abound about long-term and short-term (or working) memory, of conscious declarative and unconscious implicit memory. It is frankly impossible to do them full justice here, and they must await more detailed investigation by scholars of PR.

The most obvious contact with PR is where individual memory encounters collective, group memory – and there must always be contact between the two. Messages are easier to preserve and proselytize by people or machines grouped in an organization. The organizational memory 'cloud' can feel as integral to individuality as personal memory. It 'is situated within a larger culture or group which, in the practice of its activities, teaches its members to use memory in a particular way' (Weldon & Bellinger, 1997, p. 1161). It is a 'social phenomenon' (Weldon et al., 1997, p. 1161) as well as an individual process, able to take physical forms and decide real outcomes. Messages about products, nations, famous people, issues and policies pour unceasingly from group to person. The volume of collective memory is hard for an individual to manage; harder still to reverse the flow and insert individual memory into the group, except in the case of individuals who achieve prominence. Group memory might be communicated to individuals in different ways: simply by presenting factual reminders, by storytelling, or by collaborative exchange of recollections. The methods may be applied by a family, volunteer group, business, brand or government. They need not be perfect aides to memory, for memory itself is imperfect. Perfected memory might erase distinctions between long- and short-term recall, which would radically change the things PR does and the kinds of people who do it. Less interpretation of facts or feelings would be needed, or creative ideas for shaping memory. In our imperfect circumstances, a belief that collective is more credible than individual memory, whether true or not, gives group communication extra authority.

Memory is imperfect, and so is its public distribution (Weldon et al., 1997, p. 1161). First, the impressions of an organization may reach individuals at different times, or in the same way at the same time, with different results. Second, one person may receive the group memory more directly than another. Third, the content of the memory may change according to the individuals involved. Fourth, the media used may vary, making the medium not only the message but also part of the memory – the medium is the memory. Finally, memory can change according to individual circumstances, because PR uses time in different in ways. While distributing a message happens in present time, it is done so that past memory will align to immediate actions or future perceptions of an idea, person or object.

Weldon's and Bellinger's experiments on several forms of memory 'demonstrated the importance of social factors in cognitive performance, factors which historically have been ignored in experimental cognitive psychology' (Weldon et al., 1997, p. 1173). Social factors also illuminate another PR role for organizations: control by substituting ostensibly (but not actually) 'strong' group memory for ostensibly 'weak' individual memory.

> Whereas one might predict that collaborative recall should enhance individual recall by providing additional retrieval cues, in fact collaboration actually inhibited individual performance.
>
> (Weldon et al., 1997, p. 1173)

Collaborative recall is a group deciding a memory. It has attracted a great deal of research, partly because of its implications for accuracy, community and individual freedom of choice. It is surely correct to say that we place value on this process as 'our social contexts may be an important component of what and how we remember' (Harris, Barnier & Sutton, 2013, p. 183). The social context in memory is where PR's intervention occurs. At another level, the collaborative element may be affected by preconditions for memory retrieval, producing a perception or memory that may seem collaborative and freely or naturally reached but is in fact adulterated by the accepted preconditions. PR may for instance use 'framing' to influence collaborative recall. Hallahan defines it persuasively 'as a window or portrait frame drawn around information that delimits the subject matter and, thus, focuses attention on key elements within' (Hallahan, 1999, p. 207). PR in this way guides memory by channelling and confining it, by containing perceptions (which may be a way of remembering something) and generating cues within certain bounds that are legitimate or helpful to an organization. Framing shared memory can also make power relations because the controlling parameters are communicated by persons grouped inside organizations to consenting, resisting or unsure individuals. As far as possible, then, the media preferred in this activity is media shared by a group, for example on the grounds that – in an echo of McLuhan (see Chapter 1): 'Oral culture is social. Literate culture encourages individualism' (Tuan, 1982, p. 134). A perception of a person, event, product or organization must be framed, shaped collaboratively within the frame, and in this way absorbed by the individual.

Reason and PR

Why can PR influence reason? Little attention is paid to PR's impact on reason. To some a positive impact seems unlikely. Reason should reject PR's blandishments. It is treated with respect as a disciplined process, a mark of higher civilization, a thinking discipline which advances human development, reduces the uncertainties and indiscipline of emotion, relies on logic and fact based findings – particularly numerical ones. These guard reason against attempts to adulterate it with sense-inspired special effects. So too does reason's connection to scientific method, and through that to technical and material achievement. Many people who seem qualified to speak about the subject – scholars, scientists and the professional classes in general – equate reason with higher truths, discounting other influences on perception as irrational and often outright dangerous. To adapt the meme used by Jacob Bronowski (see Chapter 2) it is after all only a step from 'reason' to 'reasonable'; and a short and more turbulent step from 'emotion' to 'emotional'. 'It is not the business of reason to generate emotions' wrote the Philosopher Bertrand Russell in 1930. For him, one function of reason was to prevent unhelpful emotions (Russell, 2015, Part 1).

Yet not everyone has revered reason. In the late eighteenth and nineteenth century, the Romantic Movement was a reaction to the Age of Reason which had led to the Enlightenment, which led to the horrors of Revolution, war, anarchy and the squalor of industrialism. Blake, de Maistre, Beethoven, Byron, Carlyle, Henri Bergson and many others down to the present do not think reason produces higher truth. To its critics reason was unnatural; tainted by disaster and discontent; skewed towards subduing the spirit.

Bertrand Russell showed some caution about taking Reason too far. He referenced the impossibility of achieving an exact circle despite the persistent mathematical belief in 'eternal' *and* 'exact' truths. The inherent flaws in the circle suggest that 'exact reasoning applies to ideal as opposed to sensible objects':

> It is natural to go further, and to argue that thought is nobler than sense, and the objects of thought more real than those of sense-perception.
>
> (Russell, 1992, p. 56)

Caution aside, reason has established itself an inherent, if fragile, individual faculty. It is used to discern an eternal world 'revealed to the intellect but not to the senses' (Russell, 1992, p. 56). Can PR affect it? Is individual reason an obstacle or an asset to its work?

These questions raise interesting parallels between reason and memory. Individual reason shares one feature with memory. It often includes a collaborative component that like memory brings it within range of groups, and inevitably organizations. PR can access individual reason by collaborative activity, and by two other routes charted in Immanuel Kant's *Critique of Pure Reason* (1781). Kant recognized the effect of exterior objects on the individual's inner world. At the same time he recognized the value of intuition, without which true self-knowledge is impossible since all that we experience is ourselves. However, Kant did join exterior and interior experience by proposing:

> We can therefore have no knowledge of any object as thing in itself, but only in so far as it is an object of sensible intuition, that is, an appearance.
>
> (Kant, 1965, p. 127)

From this position the effect of PR on reason is clear. A thing is not immune from individual perception, so individual reasoning cannot shake off the facts of the outside world.

What form might PR's communion with reason take? Dolinina (2001) built on Kant and examined some neurology behind two possible sources for reason using the activity of reasoning: 'theoretical' and 'empirical'. Brain activity for each suggests: 'both mechanisms of reasoning are present in the brain simultaneously, but each of them is controlled by different hemispheres' (Dolinina, 2001, p. 117). Second, a review of existing research indicated that empirical reasoning was strongest in 'prelogical, traditional, "inductive"' settings, and theoretical more common in 'logical, formal, "deductive"' settings (Dolinina, 2001, p. 131).

This is helpful although from a PR viewpoint scientific research into reason can appear confining. In science Reason is a process – reasoning – used to find solutions to technical or cognitive problems, or to learn the nature of physical objects. Research necessarily concentrates on one particular problem, where there may be a real possibility of finding the absolute truth of the matter. PR rarely takes its audiences to an absolute truth, offering instead a convincing possible truth. This process is less understood: how reason is affected when choosing among different kinds of truths differently presented by competing organizations which may create a mood rather than a definitive answer. Chapter 2 described how PR moves in a more ambiguous realm where final answers are rare, persuasion continual and knowledge is insufficiently satisfying. None of this means PR ignores the individual's desire to apply reason even in opaque situations.

PR's intervention in reason is located by the observation that 'reasoning may be discovered in all sorts of symbolic action – nondiscursive as well as discursive' (Fisher, 1984, p. 1). Since reason however objective cannot avoid the individual's internal sensory experience, it cannot avoid PR. Reason itself is not immune from ourselves, to paraphrase Kant, and so the reasoning process is open to intervention from the individual, whose senses are in turn open to the external world. Through that portal PR influences theoretical and empirical reasoning processes, not only emotion. In these circumstances Kant unsurprisingly viewed reason as 'very far from having entered upon the secure path of a science, and is indeed a merely random groping' (Kant, 1965, p. 17). Pure reason lay out of reach, but the effort to understand and use it properly was underway. It could not be made alone. Kant did not think individual reason should impose itself without reference to groups:

> Kant would have one not simply rule himself, but commit instead to the autonomy of reason arising out of the deliberation of the larger community of which he is one part.
>
> (Jackson, 2007, p. 338)

It is interesting that Kant also wished to educate the individual so reason could function in cooperation with the larger community (Frierson, 2003). Eighty or so years later J. S. Mill's great essay *On Liberty* (1859) advocated education to proof the individual against the dangers of public opinion expressed in the media of his day (Mill, 1977). To some extent at least, Kant and Mill wanted reason to enrich the collective impact on thought. They wanted the reverse as well: reason itself must be influenced by the collective. It is part of this process that PR uses myth, symbols, and as we shall see more science on behalf of groups, to rouse some apparently objective qualities of individual reason. The activity complements PR's better-known appeal to features of individual emotion.

Emotion and PR

Von Mises stated that in social cooperation 'economics provides all the information required for an ultimate decision between reason and unreason' (von Mises,

1949/1966, p. 91). If this was literally correct, the individual would summon less aid from elsewhere, and PR would employ fewer means for interpreting information. Emotion is a resource used by PR to reconcile exterior and interior experience. The individual is offered a predictable, regulated, consistent exterior perception that elides with what one psychologist calls the 'roiling interior life' of the 'private individual who feels doubt, anxiety, inhibition and ambivalence that he or she may not let wholly come to the surface' (Dunning, 2013, p. 417). Crisis and issues PR are two dramatic points of contact between individual emotion and exterior events, where the need to 'understand and then control the emotional contagion among multiple publics has been a haunting challenge' (Jin & Cameron, 2004, p. 6).

For organizations, controlling 'emotional contagion' is to correct and direct it by supplying convincing information if not absolute truth. The psychologist Victor Frankl built on the existentialist Søren Kierkegaard when he suggested: 'as long as absolute truth is not accessible to us (and it never will be) relative truths have to function as mutual correctives' (Frankl, 1986, Preface to the Third Edition). Arrangements of exterior experience for a person, institution or product for example might influence 'roiling interior life' by offering a convincing relative truth; a stable rationale for its contacts with exterior experience to productively channel relevant emotions. Society generally accepts, and sometimes fears, that what McLuhan in 1964 called 'the inner life of the feelings and emotions' can be 'structured and ordered and analyzed' (McLuhan et al., 2013, Chapter 20) – and therefore directed.

Sustained scientific analysis of emotion is more recent, and often ancillary to other topics. Nevertheless contemporary neurological research links emotion to a sense of self, expressed as a theory of mind, with the participation of two neural systems in the brain. The 'mirror neuron system (MNS) co-activates actions, intention and emotions of both the self and others' (Kreplin & Fairclough, 2015, p. 5, *passim*). The 'Default Mode Network' (DMN) is associated with 'mind-wandering' and related to 'spontaneous thought' (Andrews-Hanna, 2012, Introduction):

> Humans engage in spontaneous thought with an astoundingly high frequency. Daily experience sampling techniques estimate that humans spend between 30–50% of daily life engaged in thoughts unrelated to the immediate task at hand.
> (Andrews-Hanna, 2012, The adaptive role of the default network)

Perhaps the connections between mind-wandering and free association with ideas could be fruitfully studied by PR scholars and practitioners. Perhaps it is also relevant that research finds 'the DMN may be activated during cognitive empathy or simulation of the mental state of another' (Kreplin & Fairclough, 2015, p. 5, *passim*). Related to the process are two areas of the brain, the posterior cingulate cortex and the anterior medial prefrontal cortex which 'become engaged when individuals reference information to themselves or reflect on personal preferences, beliefs, values, feelings, abilities, and physical attributes as well as engage in personal moral dilemmas' (Andrews-Hanna, 2012, The aMPFC and PCC hubs; *passim*).

Popular notions of emotion in the public arena, and therefore of many PR activities, are somewhat cruder. This does not make them any less influential. Emotion (sometimes called 'affect' by researchers) has been described as 'the flavor of information and knowledge' (Sørensen, Thellefsen & Thellefsen, 2016, p. 21) and like marketing PR uses 'emotion-evoking stimuli in persuasive communication' (Hasford, Hardesty & Kidwell, 2015, p. 836), and often heavily depends on it. Writing in 1952, Bernays thought PR practitioners should 'be fully aware of available knowledge about emotion'. Nor was it 'a contradiction to stress both scientific knowledge and emotion' (Bernays, 1980, p. 133). Connections between emotion and reason are more urgent in light of the Information Revolution and as we shall see PR's unstoppable biotechnological future, in which 'an emotion-driven tactic relying more on broadcast and electronic media might evoke deeper arousal and understanding' (Jin et al., 2006, p. 21).

It scarcely need be said PR's uses of emotion are varied. Tempestuous agitation is not its only manifestation. PR is not a broker for passion, discarding reason altogether. Nevertheless there is a tendency to overlook Bernays' advice. Emotion was often treated by critics of PR as a distasteful, dangerous, untechnocratic topic to be avoided or minimized in practical communication, especially in the era of social media irresponsibility. Reasoning and communicating nevertheless continue to seek out symbols that arouse public feeling. Emotion and reason can be aligned in PR, which has always used receptacles of feeling such as sports arenas, religious venues, children or money. It might seek to convey certain emotional characteristics of its clients, whether entertainment celebrities, politicians, or particular brands and products. Many PR activities in these areas might certainly be concerned with the generation of *strong* emotion. Others are not, and instead concentrate on generating *appropriate* emotion within the individual nervous system.[2]

PR's work to align emotion with reason is part of a familiar communication activity:

> Interdependent, interactive interrelations working within every process of meaning creation, beginning with information and going through experience and emotion finding the way to thoughts and concepts leading to knowledge.
>
> (Sørensen et al., 2016, pp. 21–22)

What elements of emotion are helpful to PR?

Emotion as 'truth'

Where it relates to PR, early quantitative communication research provided evidence for the view that 'emotion affects the meaning given a communicated message' (Porterfield, 1976, p. 11). In 1972 Pettit et al. postulated that 'introspection' – 'an inward look at one's feelings, thoughts, and emotions' had an important part to play in 'perception and language use' at higher levels (Pettit, 1972, p. 38).

Newer research on emotion has tended to neglect PR, but the overall body of literature is vast and often connects to PR it concentrates on psychology and neuroscience. Recent psychological study appears to support the instinctive sense that emotion is more than the sum of what may appear irrational parts. Emotion contains the quality of 'psychological essentialism' – the idea of an essential reality and truth. It can communicate 'the inference that categories have consistent, diagnostic, surface features and a metaphysical essence that makes them what they are' (Lindquist, Gendron, Oosterwijk & Barrett, 2013, p. 629). This naturally makes emotions an interface between the individual and external experience. They are a measure individuals may use to interpret the truth of an experience and discover if the interpretation is shared by others. They work this way because the individual can 'automatically and effortlessly perceive emotions in other people and in nonhuman animals as easily as we read words on a page' (Lindquist et al., 2013, p. 629). Emotions thus become a medium for conveying information, and also the essential context of that information including whether others share the same feelings. Lindquist et al. reported that emotion was not necessarily confined to purely individual experience. It could contain 'essentialism' and act as a heuristic 'that does not necessarily accurately represent the nature of emotion as measured in momentary emotional experiences' (Lindquist et al., 2013, p. 640). If emotion has an essential universal 'essence' inevitably it will be used to reach the individual at a fundamentally persuasive level. Emotion is:

> Recognized by mental machinery that is innately hardwired, reflexive and universal, so that all people everywhere (barring organic disturbance) are born in possession of five or six perceptually grounded emotion categories.
>
> (Barrett, Lindquist & Gendron, 2007)

Emotion does not evaporate once the individual apparently applies reason to achieve understanding, which is to say the 'truth' of something. Sørensen et al. persuasively emphasize as much in a study of meaning creation: 'As we gradually attach more characteristics to the object, the knowledge level becomes the dominant one, but it still contains emotions' (Sørensen et al., 2016, p. 31).

Emotion as contagion

Reason is less contagious than emotion. If emotion were not contagious PR would use it less. The contagion of emotion is adaptable to a place, issue or product in a way helpful to those communicating for an organization.

Emotional contagion is a historical phenomenon attracting attention for instance in crowds, war, mobs or spectator sports. It has drawn less attention in PR. Fortunately, other research helps us understand how and why PR uses it.

The idea of emotional 'contagion' must be handled with care. Emotion might always 'roil' or it might not, but some value it. To the prominent German philosopher J. G. Hamann (1730–88) it was the essence of our creativeness and humanness, whereby: 'To resist emotion with logical distinctions is to try and stop the ocean wave with a barrier of sand' (Berlin, 1965, p. 2). Others were more sceptical but recognized its force. Charles Mackay's Victorian bestseller *Extraordinary Popular Delusions and the Madness of Crowds* (1841), Gustav Le Bon's *The Crowd: A Study of the Popular Mind* (1895), Wilfred Trotter's *Instincts of the Herd in Peace and War* (1916) helped establish the way emotion in public domain is often treated today, as 'moral epidemics' suffered by communities so obsessed with a subject that they 'go mad in its pursuit' (Mackay, 1995, pp. xvi–xvii). When the individual is part of the crowd, Le Bon remarked, we see:

> The disappearance of the conscious personality, the predominance of the unconscious personality, the turning of feelings and ideas in an identical direction by means of suggestion and contagion.
>
> (Le Bon, 2001, p. 8)

When and how is emotion contagious? It has many carriers, human and material. 'Infection' may spread by forceful concentration on a single false, true or unproven idea. A study of emotion-driven messages about one product noted that effect: 'emotions need to be merely accessible in memory from thoughts of another product to influence unrelated judgments' (Hasford et al., 2015, p. 844). Alternatively, emotional contagion can be generated collectively. Experiments with Facebook and other social media participants support the idea that emotions spread by other media, in this case online and 'in absence of non-verbal cues typical of in-person interaction' (Ferrara & Yang, 2015, p. 1; Kramer, Guillory & Hancock, 2014). One Facebook experiment produced early evidence backing 'previously contested claims that emotions spread through contagion on a network' (Kramer et al., 2014, p. 8789). Another 20-year health study found happiness can be communicated through networks of people, concluding in terms that seem to fit PR's current *modus operandi* if we use its initials in place of 'clinical or policy':

> To the extent that clinical or policy manoeuvres increase the happiness of one person, they might have cascade effects on others, thereby enhancing the efficacy and cost effectiveness of the intervention.
>
> (Fowler, Christakis, Steptoe & Diez Roux, 2009, p. 26)

Besides an ability to spread across media 'petri dishes', emotional contagion has 'languages' at its disposal. The oldest among them must include the language communicated by the human face. Barrett et al. reviewed 'evidence for the role of language in emotion perception' (2007) between the human face as interpreted by the observing human mind:

Emotion perception is shaped by the external context that a face inhabits and by the internal context that exists in the mind of the perceiver during an instance of perception.

(Barrett et al., 2007, Implications)

This language of emotion, this meeting of external experience and internal interpretation, is affected by other sensations including: 'color perception, the visualization of spatial locations, time perception' (Barrett et al., 2007, Implications). Kuperman, Estes, Brysbaert and Warriner examined words, finding spoken word recognition was affected by 'arousal' ('the extent to which a stimulus is calming or exciting') and 'valence' ('the extent to which a stimulus is negative or positive') (Kuperman et al., 2014, p. 1065). On a larger scale, organizations also use space, time, colour and words to arouse emotion.

Despite its preoccupation with the group over the individual, PR's use of emotion's contagious qualities to evoke 'truth' has more implications for individuality than groups. Contagious emotion is the result of sensitized individual emotions. From his study of rumours the early neurosurgeon and social psychologist Wilfred Trotter observed that a 'strong stimulus to herd instinct' causes the individual to feel 'maximal sensitiveness to his fellows':

To their presence or absence, their alarms and braveries, and in no less degree to their opinions.

(Trotter, 1916, p. 144)

These conditions generate strong communication between individuals in loose groups and more tightly structured organizations. Alongside the organizations themselves this awareness of other individuals in their particular organizational identities deepens the emotionally 'infected' individual's need for PR.

Such immense communication potential obliges PR to consider the individual in whom the emotion actually resides. PR shows its dependence on individuals by transferring emotion from their bodies into other media. Nevertheless, an individual's emotions are only valuable to PR when she or he belongs to a group and at no other time. For a little longer, Bernays' hard words from 1923 may still – just – hold true: 'The group and the herd are the basic mechanisms of public change' (Bernays, 1961, p. 111).

It is suggested later that this situation is about to change. At this time it is fair to say that when PR presents exterior impressions that engage the individual's inner life it is trying to attach part of that individual's individuality to the ambitions of a group. The invitation is delivered by creating a personal relationship between it and the mind, by using the contagious qualities of emotion, by aligning it to the subjective processes of reasoning, and by shaping a memory of something to make it seem universally true.

'The central challenge of science in the twenty-first century is to understand the human mind in biological terms' wrote the neuropsychiatrist and Nobel Prize winner Eric Kandel (Kandel, 2012, Preface). PR may not contribute overmuch to that task, but that task is essential to understanding PR. Some of the research discussed here helps us glimpse how PR connects to the inner life of fully evolved human beings. Memory, reason and emotion carry PR into human individuality. There is a biological relationship between them all, akin to 'an emotional neuroaesthetic', a phrase Kandel uses to describe 'our perceptual, emotional, and empathetic responses to works of art' (Kandel, 2012, Preface).

For the individual and for PR, inner life must synthesize PR's appeals to our memory, reason and emotion. The results for the individual and those whom PR represents can be constructive, if unequal. For either or both groups, the relationship is one way to gratify that inner urge for truth described earlier. PR uses many methods and media to do its work, but as Victor Frankl wrote: 'Approaching the one truth from various sides, sometimes even in opposite directions, we cannot attain it, but we may at least encircle it' (Frankl, 1986, Preface to the Third Edition).

This book seeks to learn why individuality is encircled by PR. Chapter 2 was about the roots of our desire for what is currently called PR. Chapter 3 is about the ways that desire satisfies our inner life. Chapter 4 will be about a third component of our individuality that explains the individual's deep connection to PR: our wish to exercise power, to have power exercised over us, and to communicate our experiences with it to other individuals inside groups.

Notes

1 The phrase is from Wittgenstein's famous last sentence to *Tractatus Logico-Philosophicus*. Many questions today have usually been asked yesterday. This is no exception and shows how much the subject matters to humanity.
2 Jin and Cameron's pioneering discussion of PR and emotion acknowledged PR's nuanced approach by using 'affect' as an 'umbrella for a set of more specific mental processes include emotions, moods, and sometimes attitudes' (Jin et al., 2006, p. 9). I do find these categories helpful but use the more familiar term 'emotion' on behalf of all three, since much research uses affect and emotion interchangeably.

References

Andrews-Hanna, J. R. (2012). The brain's default network and its adaptive role in internal mentation. *The Neuroscientist*, *18*(3), 251–270. Retrieved from www.ncbi.nlm.nih.gov/pmc/articles/PMC3553600/.

Barrett, L. F., Lindquist, K. A., & Gendron, M. (2007). Language as context for the perception of emotion. *Trends in Cognitive Sciences*, *11*(8), 327–332. Retrieved from www.ncbi.nlm.nih.gov/pmc/articles/PMC2225544/.

Berlin, I. (1965). Two enemies of the Enlightenment. 2. The First Onslaught: J. G. Hamann and his Disciples. Woodbridge Lectures, Columbia University, NY: 25–28 October. Retrieved from http://berlin.wolf.ox.ac.uk/lists/nachlass/hamann.pdf.

Bernays, E. L. (1961). *Crystallizing public opinion*. New York: Liveright Pub. Corp.

Bernays, E. L. (1980). *Public relations*. eBook. Norman, OK: University of Oklahoma Press.

Bernays, E. L., & Miller, M. C. (2005). *Propaganda*. eBook. Brooklyn, NY: Ig Pub.

Buck, R. (1991). Motivation, emotion and cognition: A developmental-interactionist view. *International review of studies on emotion, 1*, 101–142.

Dolinina, I. B. (2001). 'Theoretical' and 'Empirical' reasoning modes from the Neurological perspective. *Argumentation, 15*(2), 117–134.

Dunning, D. (2013). The paradox of knowing. *Psychologist, 26*(6), 414–417.

Ellsworth, P. C. (1991). Some implications of cognitive appraisal theories of emotion. *International review of studies on emotion, 1*, 143–161.

Ferrara, E., & Yang, Z. (2015). Measuring emotional contagion in social media. *PLOS one, 10*(11), e0142390.

Fisher, W. R. (1984). Narration as a human communication paradigm: The case of public moral argument. *Communications Monographs, 51*(1), 1–22.

Fowler, J., Christakis, N., Steptoe, & Diez Roux. (2009). Dynamic spread of happiness in a large social network: Longitudinal analysis of the Framingham heart study social network. *BMJ: British Medical Journal, 338*(7685), 23–27. Retrieved from www.jstor.org/stable/20511686.

Frankl, V. E. (1986). *The doctor and the soul: From psychotherapy to logotherapy.* eBook. New York: Vintage Books.

Frierson, P. (2003). *Freedom and anthropology in Kant's moral philosophy.* Cambridge: Cambridge University Press.

Hallahan, K. (1999). Seven models of framing: Implications for public relations. *Journal of Public Relations Research, 11*(3), 205–242.

Harris, C. B., Barnier, A. J., & Sutton, J. (2013). Shared encoding and the costs and benefits of collaborative recall. *Journal of Experimental Psychology: Learning, Memory, and Cognition, 39*(1), 183–195. doi:10.1037/a0028906.

Hasford, J., Hardesty, D. M., & Kidwell, B. (2015). More than a feeling: emotional contagion effects in persuasive communication. *Journal of Marketing Research, 52*(6), 836–847.

Jackson, L. (2007). The Individualist? The autonomy of reason in Kant's philosophy and educational views. *Studies in Philosophy and Education, 26*(4), 335–344.

Jin, Y., & Cameron, G. (2004). Rediscovering Emotion in Public Relations: An Adapted Appraisal Model and An Emotion Laden Contingency Plane. *Conference Papers – International Communication Association, 1.*

Kandel, E. R. (2012). *The age of insight: The quest to understand the unconscious in art, mind, and brain: from Vienna 1900 to the present.* eBook. New York: Random House.

Kant, I. (1965). *Critique of pure reason.* New York: St. Martin's Press.

Kramer, A. D., Guillory, J. E., & Hancock, J. T. (2014). Experimental evidence of massive-scale emotional contagion through social networks. *Proceedings of the National Academy of Sciences, 111*(24), 8788–8790.

Kreplin, U., & Fairclough, S. H. (2015). Effects of self-directed and other-directed introspection and emotional valence on activation of the rostral prefrontal cortex during aesthetic experience. *Neuropsychologia, 71*, 38–45. doi:10.1016/j.neuropsychologia.2015.03.013. Retrieved from https://curve.coventry.ac.uk/open/file/55792cb2-60af-4dd0-9a60-ee36e764db4d/1/Effects%20of.pdf.

Kuperman, V., Estes, Z., Brysbaert, M., & Warriner, A. B. (2014). Emotion and language: Valence and arousal affect word recognition. *Journal of Experimental Psychology: General, 143*(3), 1065–1081.

Lao Tzu., & Lau, D. C. (2012). *Tao te ching.* eBook. London: Penguin Books.

Le Bon, G. (2001). *The crowd: A study of the popular mind.* Mineola, NY: Dover Publications.

Lindquist, K. A., Gendron, M., Oosterwijk, S., & Barrett, L. F. (2013). Do people essentialize emotions? Individual differences in emotion essentialism and emotional experience. *Emotion, 13*(4), 629.

Mackay, C. (1995). *Extraordinary popular delusions & the madness of crowds.* New York: Crown Trade Paperbacks.

McLuhan, M., & Gordon, W. T. (2013). *Understanding media: The extensions of man.* New York: Gingko Press.

Mill, J. S. (1977). On Liberty. In Edited by J. M. Robson. Introduction by A. Brady. *The collected works of John Stuart Mill*, Volume XVIII. Toronto: University of Toronto Press, London: Routledge and Kegan Paul. Retrieved from http://oll.libertyfund.org/?option=com_staticxt&staticfile=show.php%3Fcollection=46&Itemid=27.

von Mises, L. (1949/1966). *Human action: A treatise on economics.* Third Edition. Chicago: Regnery.

Neisser, U. (1967). *Cognitive psychology.* New York: Appleton-Century-Crofts.

Pettit, J. D. (1972). Guidelines and suggestions for research in business communication. *Journal of Business Communication, 9*(3), 37–60. Retrieved from http://journals.sagepub.com/doi/pdf/10.1177/002194367200900304.

Porterfield, C. D. (1976). The effects of emotion and communication skill on message meaning. *Journal of Business Communication, 13*(3), 3–14.

Raichle, M. E. (2015). The restless brain: how intrinsic activity organizes brain function. *Phil. Trans. R. Soc. B, 370*(1668), 20140172. Retrieved from http://rstb.royalsociety publishing.org/content/370/1668/20140172.

Russell, B. (1930/2015). *The conquest of happiness.* eBook. Philadelphia, PA: R. P. Pryne.

Russell, B. (1992). *History of Western philosophy.* Abingdon, Oxon: Routledge.

Sørensen, B., Thellefsen, T., & Thellefsen, M. (2016). The meaning creation process, information, emotion, knowledge, two objects, and significance-effects: Some Peircean remarks. *Semiotica, 2016*(208), 21–33.

Teske, J. A. (2001). Cognitive neuroscience, temporal ordering, and the human spirit. *Zygon®, 36*(4), 667–678.

Trotter, W. (1916). *Instincts of the herd in peace and war.* London: Fisher Unwin.

Tuan, Y. F. (1982). *Segmented worlds and self: A study of group life and individual consciousness.* Minneapolis, MN: University of Minnesota Press.

Weldon, M. S., & Bellinger, K. D. (1997). Collective memory: collaborative and individual processes in remembering. *Journal of Experimental Psychology: Learning, Memory, and Cognition, 23*(5), 1160–1175.

Zhang, D., & Raichle, M. (2010). Disease and the brain's dark energy. *Nature Reviews. Neurology* [serial online]. January 2010; 6(1):15–28.

4   PR, power and neuroscience

PR and power: common origins

The last two chapters suggested the function now named PR was not forced on unwilling individuals. If PR were abolished today it would immediately reappear under a different name. It is worth repeating that the individual has an inherent need for it, which joined to a need to survive and flourish in groups elevates PR into a desire catalyzed by evolutionary characteristics described in Chapter 2. Another fundamental subject needs attention: whether the individual also desires PR because 'He is remarkably susceptible to leadership' (Trotter, 1916, p. 114). What might power suggest about PR and individuality? That is the subject of this chapter.

Power may be latent, but must be expressed if it is to act in human affairs. Friedrich Nietzsche touched on 'natural' power's junction with communication in 1887 when he wrote: 'all "happening" in the organic world consists of overpowering and dominating, and again all overpowering and domination is a new interpretation and adjustment' (Nietzsche & Samuel, 2003, Essay II). Less poetically than Nietzsche, more scientifically, and equally accurately it has been written 'for primates, a key factor creating structure within the social environment is power' (Hogeveen, Inzlicht & Obhi, 2013, p. 755). A third factor shared by all primates is power's evolutionary link to status, which must be displayed to be asserted and desired:

> Major components of human status, including competence, attraction to experts, prestige, power, hubristic pride, and (possibly) authentic pride, are homologous phenomena between humans and primates, and […] they can be traced back to the competitive and cooperative aspects of primate dominance.
>
> (Chapais, 2015, p. 163)

It is not surprising that PR can bring the individual into power relations with organizations. Mistaken ideas that PR plays a subordinate role are surprising. Almost down to the present, there was a tendency to view managed public communication (if they noticed it at all) as the echo for a more powerful force (which in this case is power itself), winningly amplifying its requirements much as a court poet, bard, minstrel, scop or skald did for a ruler.

Plato's Socrates was not one of the political, religious or economic rulers of fifth century Athens. His own considerable public status depended on the communication of ideas by himself and his followers. It is not known if this affected his view of public communication using poetry, songs, noble lies and ritual as a servant of the all-wise guardians in Plato's *Republic*, but for him it was an essential servant. A refined version of Socrates' approach was taken by the ideal, spiritually perfected head of the perfect state envisaged by the important Arab thinker Abu Nasr Al-Farabi (*c.* AD 875–950/1), who had read Plato extensively. Al-Farabi supposed that when power was communicated from a single source of perfect Truth, managed public communication vanishes from the scene. Communication might exist without artifice, in its purest possible form (Al-Farabi & Walzer, 1985).

Even in imperfect societies social truths might emerge and germinate without communication artifice. The philosopher G. W. F. Hegel (1770–1831) lectured in the early nineteenth century on 'the spirit of events' which was apparently created by means not fully explained and in charge of its own communication. It was self-aware, possessing 'consciousness of its own ends and interests' and knowledge of 'the way in which it interprets itself to others and acts on their powers of representation in order to manipulate their will' (Hegel et al., 2010, p. 13).

A more useful possibility than all these is that power originates in biology, is magnified by organizations and inextricably dependent on communication. Managed public communication is not necessarily subordinate or the outcome of spiritual forces beyond conventional analysis, or natural forces beyond human control. Power is instead a partner with PR because the individual feels biologically rewarded by power-based relations with groups. This possibility was suggested long before the modern era of neurological investigation. Xifra finds that for the seventeenth century philosopher Thomas Hobbes:

> The individual is not an autonomous, closed, independent entity. He suffers from the company of others, but he needs this company to know the value of his self and enjoy the pleasures of domination and excellence.
>
> (Xifra, 2017, p. 4)

Connections between power, the group and power communication attracted much closer attention in the nineteenth century. Public communication techniques evolved as power-holders in civil life and commerce sought more from subordinated individuals: more production and consumption, skills, education, forms of service, ideas, goodwill or activism. The 'court of public opinion' (Bernays, 2005, p. 69) enlarged with new media to shape the spirit of events. It tightened the connections between communication and power observed by Shakespeare and Machiavelli among others, and begged a question voiced by the American social commentator Walter Lippmann (1889–1974). How, asked Lippmann, is 'Public Opinion crystallized' (Lippmann, 1997, p. 125)? In his 1921 book *Public Opinion*

Lippmann demonstrated that the era of Fordism and mass media meant 'crystallizing of a common will' (Lippmann, 1997, p. 140) could be achieved by applying techniques which established a 'practical relationship':

> Between what is in people's heads and what is out there beyond their ken in the environment.
>
> (Lippmann, 1997, p. 125)

To this end: 'Because of their transcendent practical importance' and 'power to siphon emotion out of distinct ideas' (Lippmann, 1997, pp. 150, 151):

> No successful leader has ever been too busy to cultivate the symbols which organize his following.
>
> (Lippmann, 1997, p. 150)

Lippmann caught the spirit of an era needing to preface direction by persuasion, reflecting ideas about individual autonomy ushered in by spreading consumerism and literacy, and earlier political ideas behind Jean-Jacques Rousseau's *The Social Contract* (1762). 'The strongest man', Rousseau wrote, 'is never strong enough to be master all the time, unless he transforms force into right and obedience into duty' (Rousseau & Cranston, 2004, p. 5). A distinct, managed, function was needed to crystallize power's transformative, organizing symbols into a prevailing opinion using persuasion not command.

As inheritor of that function, PR is often urged to recognize its ethical responsibilities and cultivate more open and equal relations between less powerful people and more powerful organizations. It is broadly or at least publicly agreed in many (not all) parts of the world that 'empowerment' is what society demands and needs. It is observed, surely rightly, that: 'Organizational scholars and practitioners have become increasingly aware of the benefits of authentic self-expression in organizations' (Hewlin, Dumas & Burnett, 2017, p. 179), instead of 'facades of conformity' (Hewlin et al., 2017, p. 178 *passim*).

Neuroscience and psychology so far support the view that reducing power-based relations enhances an individual's executive functions (in the sense of cognitive alertness) (Guinote, 2007; Smith, Jostmann, Galinsky & van Dijk, 2008). But such views are challenged by the ways communicated power can be actually received by individuals, and not by an agglomerate 'public opinion' and those who claim to lead or speak for sections of it. Desiring PR may be connected to desiring power imbalances. We have already seen that PR would be endangered if the individual was self-governed by pure reason, logic or one dominant majority opinion in the public sphere. Personal opinions about a subject would simply consist of automatic obedience to the majority view or, if reason and logic dominated, uncompromising openness to all views, public analysis of all raw data, and finally the logical identification of a correct course of civil or commercial action. PR would be equally endangered if power lost its value. This might occur if every individual in a society agreed on what openness and equality actually meant, found a way to abolish power-based structures, and then settled for nothing less than equality in all their relations with all organizations. In such a world individuals would be less open to the crafts of persuasion or power projection.

In the world as it is, however, communicating power continues to matter. Reason, openness, monopolies of opinion and equality are a long way from supplanting PR, whose expansion across subjects, time and spaces shows individuals seek something else from organizations that opens minds to subjective opinions, inherited habits and customs, and biology. These encourage us to follow people, products and organizations which do not – cannot – use social equality to strengthen their position. Such circumstances reinforce the conditions for personal subordination to power. A growing body of neurological research confirms 'a reliable relationship between power and information processing style' (Hogeveen et al., 2013, p. 755), which must shape the way information is delivered as well as processed. As these findings apply to individual nervous systems, so too they should apply to the organizations individuals create.

Lippmann's 'practical relationship', mediated by PR, invariably mirrors such inequities. Far from resenting inequities, individuals often accept them, and actively desire to be in structures dominated by others. They do so for buying, selling or believing, or for larger social benefits offered in a large civic 'society'. Such common activities are suffused with a sense of identity over which power-holders seek leadership, occasionally to the point of ownership, sometimes eliding into a myth of infallibility. These natural, inherent and highly individual tendencies contribute to the hierarchical structure of organizations from distant past to present, including those wishing to abolish hierarchies altogether. Thinkers and agitators from Confucius and Al-Farabi to Robert Owen and Lenin; political leaders from Menes to Mao; businesses from Genda Shigyō to Apple grasped the value of cultivating hierarchy within an organization to supportive or at least non-resisting audiences.

We must separate such power communication from the supporting act of distracting people *apropos* Juvenal's satirical remark about bread and circuses, and from similar Marxian pronouncements about religion as 'opium of the people' and 'illusory happiness' (Marx, 1992, 'Contribution to the Critique'). Beneath the 'diversions' such PR satisfies the civic or commercial wishes of many individuals who willingly collaborate in being led; building on the not infrequent individual wish to shed responsibility by ceding particular actions or decisions to someone, something or somewhere else.

Individuals seeking to be led today still join the kinds of crowds studied by Le Bon, Kierkegaard, Mackay, Lenin and others described in Chapters 2 and 3; or join global or local communities online, coalescing on new media ostensibly valued as platforms of a more equal, civic-minded society. In both cases, in groups large or small, there are individuals submitting to the communicated authority of majority opinion and its leaders, or to 'resistance' leaders. It is an age-old trait long discussed and researched by some including J. S. Mill in *On Liberty* (1859) or Solomon Asch (1951) along with those just named.

Communicating conformity

In the public domain today, if not in the private, the word 'conformity' is not entirely popular. This individual is often encouraged (at least publicly) not to conform; to 'disrupt' conventional thinking in the belief that: 'High integrity leaders should communicate clearly that dissension is good for the organization' (Hewlin et al., 2017, p. 193). How does this sit with the realities of holding and communicating power? Historically, communicating conformity has been encouraged in the public sphere. The ideal states of Confucius and Plato made a virtue of it. In 1651 Hobbes' recommended that the 'Sovereign Representative' of a state should use communication to enforce his position and secure conformity, by discouraging resistance:

> It is against his duty, to let the people be ignorant, or misinformed of the grounds, and reasons of those his essentiall [*sic*] Rights.
>
> (Hobbes, 2012, Chapter 30)

PR is used to encourage conformity around a subject so products might sell, ideas might be acted on, or groups might cohere, so that a society might function cooperatively and so leaders might lead. This has always been one purpose of PR and its antecedents. What is conformity in these circumstances? In the hands of PR, group conformity is not spontaneous agreement or obedience; it is a managed agreement to be obedient or to cooperate. Commands to an obedient and controlled society do not need very persuasive PR, and agreement between individuals can also happen without it. Power-centred PR wants an organization's authority to be accepted by large numbers of individuals, most of who have never met one another.

Conformity must be counted as a human survival instinct, still very much alive. It was the underlying communication objective of the first groups formed by fully developed modern humans, emerging from earlier human and animal characteristics which can be observed in the natural world today. Cooperation and survival are glued together by communicating conformity. Conformity is a reward for successful cohesion and may be 'inferred from the number and strength of mutual positive attitudes among the members of a group' (Lott & Lott, 1961, p. 408). Later research continued to support this view, especially within one of the oldest human groupings of individuals, the family. High conformity families can use communication efficiently. There is less need for self-explanation and more self-orientation. They appear to be better at interpreting, questioning and seeking advice than low-conformity families who require more 'conformation, acknowledgement, and reflection' (Koerner & Cvancara, 2002, p. 133).

Conformity may offer some neurological rewards. The individual, once in a group, undergoes a 'behavioural adjustment based on reinforcement learning mechanisms' in two areas of the brain implicated in – among other things – moderating social behaviour and reinforcement, and also reward cognition (respectively the posterior medial frontal cortex and the ventral striatum) (Schnuerch & Gibbons, 2014, p. 466).

Effectively communicated conformity produces groups (or organizations) that are more efficient than non-conforming groups. This originally was an evolutionary advantage because it helped individuals work together, and it still confers benefits. The conforming influence of family communications itself appears to strengthen or weaken later conformities, including to consumer goods (Mandrik, Fern & Bao, 2005; Moore, Wilkie & Lutz, 2002). Applied psychology provides support for this not surprising assumption. Effectively communicated conformity means taxpayers are more likely to pay taxes, charities to receive donations or household energy consumption to decrease (Stallen & Sanfey, 2014, p. 337). Again, there seems to be neural rewards for what one academic paper calls 'prosocial conduct' during social interaction between individuals (Bault, Pelloux, Fahrenfort, Ridderinkhof & van Winden, 2015, p. 877). Presumably, neural rewards are an evolutionary reward for cooperating in hierarchical groups to improve the odds of survival. Human biology at times seems to insist on conformity. Pro-social activities produce matching activity in areas of the brain that may mediate mimicry, participate in the conforming process and also in emotion and spatial memory (respectively, the medial prefrontal cortex or mPFC and the posterior cingulate cortex). Neural mimicry deserves closer attention and will receive it later. It is apparently important to the individual's inner experience of power: a link between power's successful communication and agreed subordination.

Conformity can build successful social ties, and those too offer neurological rewards. Social ties were implicated in areas of the brain connected to social perception and – significantly – the distinction of the self (respectively the bilateral posterior superior temporal sulcus – pSTS, and the temporo-parietal junction) (Bault et al., 2015). Interestingly, a legacy hypothesis suggests strong social ties outweigh an individual's diminishing personal advantage. This depends on 'an interaction partner who proved to be kind of cooperative in the past' (Bault et al., 2015, p. 882). If confirmed, it reinforces the evidence that conformity, attractively communicated, delivers a variety of neurological rewards to human individuality even when its personal benefits diminish. If strong neural bonds with individuals are communicated by organizations or their leaders, the social bonds can be maintained for a longer period at the individual level, and therefore the group level as well.

Some neural evidence, then, suggests groups are bound into conformation by individual cues, and not the other way around. Perhaps this connects to other research suggesting that societal power is frequently associated across cultures with a greater good, and greater honesty:

> The personalized power concept (vs. socialized power concept) increased (vs. decreased) the tolerance of corruption.
>
> (Wang & Sun, 2015, p. 86)

Conformity on power's behalf may show itself in corporate public affairs or brand campaigns or in attempts by opposing campaign groups to represent a 'group' identity rather than speak for any particular individual or individuality itself. No doubt those communicating to, say, 'consumers' or 'society as a whole' accept their collective approach has bigger consequences for individuality, at least for the topic being publicized. We have already seen that Edward Bernays was one communicator who felt that way. Typically, he justified his position with an almost shocking frankness rare in much public communication. His view is interesting for anyone asking why power-based PR can be accepted and desired by those using or receiving it. It appears in his first book, *Crystalizing Public Opinion*, published in 1923. The title may express an intent to answer the question raised (and phrased) in Lippmann's book two years earlier. Bernays' initial remarks on the subject are blunt:

> Public opinion is a term describing an ill-defined, mercurial and changeable group of individual judgments.
>
> (Bernays, 1961, p. 61)

As that view suggests, Bernays not surprisingly believed conformed or crystallized public opinion delivered social benefits in democracies: improved public health, increased awareness of prejudice, laws against bad driving. 'Only by mastering the techniques of communication' he wrote, 'can leadership be exercised fruitfully' (Bernays, 1947, p. 113). Bernays, like his contemporary practitioner Ivy Lee, believed that 'Propaganda' (a common, non-pejorative word for PR in the early twentieth century) overcame the 'logic-proof compartments' and 'absolutism' of the 'average citizen':

> Which prevent him from seeing in terms of experience and thought rather than in terms of group reaction.
>
> (Bernays, 1961, p. 122)

This interpretation did not see conformity as a threat to individuality, but an opportunity for the group, an aide to mutual understanding in complex societies. A practical expression of it was conducted by Bernays' contemporary Gandhi, who describes his public campaigns in the ethnically and religiously diverse British Imperial colony of South Africa and Indian Empire in his *Autobiography: The Story of My Experiments with Truth* (1925–29). When Bernays' published *Crystallizing Public Opinion* in 1923 Gandhi was in prison for his non-cooperation campaign against the British authorities in India. Both men understood how PR (which they both called 'Propaganda' at that time) might conform the individual's *membership* of a group to a particular social objective.

Conformity's practical benefits can produce ambiguous activity. PR must present the individual with a preferred choice of leaders and organizations. PR might justify power relations to individuals by making conforming emotionally attractive in order to steer the choice, even in societies where other choices are restricted. Perhaps choice provides a neural satisfaction of its own, and a real or illusory sense of *choosing* between conformities is another way for the individual to accept power-based connections with organizations. Possibly it is paradoxical, but conformity to power might be the reward for making an independent choice.

Autonomy is rewarded when part of it is given up, and conforming is the objective when hierarchies are communicated. The will to demonstrate power and the desire to conform to it takes PR deep into the human nervous system. Can we say any more about the neurological rewards of power-holding and subordination?

PR and a neuroscience of power-holding

Power for power's sake versus PR for PR's sake

As far as PR is concerned, power-holders must have strategic communication needs. They exist in businesses, politics, campaigning nonprofits, governments, community groups: any organization with resources to manage its public communication. Those leading large organizations are obvious beneficiaries of PR's deep connection to target groups. Resources, knowledge and authority to direct others are among the rewards of power, none of which can be obtained without communication. Other rewards involve the power-holder's personality. These too may be attributable to PR's effect on the nervous system, for instance in the confidence felt from increased levels of the neurotransmitter serotonin (Madsen, 1985). What is PR's role in this?

Hannah Arendt in 1950 notably wrote of 'the bourgeoisie's political device of "power for power's sake"' (Arendt, 1994, Preface), but power for its own sake is a self-contained satisfaction, does not need to be expressed and does not fully explain its public pursuit. A benefit must be experienced, which must be connected to relationships between power, individuality and PR. The need to control communication to others is often cited as a result of material ambitions (the urge to accumulate resources for instance) and not a primary motive in its own right. But power in any sphere demands a wish to communicate: to want and to wield information, whether giving subordinates directions for a task or shaping the general attitudes of organizations. Because of this, PR has rewards of its own to offer seekers after power. 'Communication for communication's sake' is a more realistic interpretation of the will to power than is power for power's sake.

Psychological and neurological bonds join power, communication and gratification. Many rewards of power, material or otherwise, are inert unless the power-holder communicates them. Here is Machiavelli's warning to princes acting with liberality:

> If one exercises it honestly and as it should be exercised, it may not become known, and you will not avoid the reproach of its opposite.
> (Machiavelli & Baker-Smith, 1992, p. 72)

Generous or mean-spirited, a power-holding individual usually wants to communicate because effective public communication expresses a desired power imbalance between individuals or organizations, presenting it as an ordained state of affairs.

Because it is inextricably joined to managing public communication, it is important to explore what is known of the neurological conditions binding power and communication to individuality. It is also important because hitherto human biological research and PR have rarely made contact, but common ground is rising between them. There is for instance some recognition that neurological research is 'shaped by historical, cultural and political-economic forces' (Vrecko, 2010, p. 1). Managed public communication plays a large part in shaping those forces, which are otherwise opaque and difficult to discern. PR research sometimes uses scientific or mathematical methodologies, believing they add insight, order and credibility to its activities, but rarely investigates purely scientific subjects, with the occasional and important exception of psychology. The neuroscience of power brings science and PR closer. The indeterminate elements of 'power and culture' oblige PR to accept that the individual encounters the communicated world via the nervous system either wholly or in part. In turn, neuroscience is invited to understand the role of power in its wider context, including:

> Existing literatures on the history and politics of psychology – particularly those that analyze formations of knowledge, power and subjectivity associated with the discipline and its practical applications.
>
> (Vrecko, 2010, p. 1)

The rewards of communicating power: fewer cues

Managed public communication must lay out the character of a power, and its responsibilities. 'No one, strictly speaking,' suggested the philosopher Michel Foucault 'has an official right to power;'

> And yet it is always exerted in a particular direction, with some people on one side and some on the other. It is often difficult to say who holds power in a precise sense, but it is easy to see who lacks power.
>
> (Foucault & Bouchard, 1981, p. 213)

PR justifies and directs the flow of information and instruction, which strengthens the power-holder's private self-image: 'Felt power is thus the mechanism linking position power to emotional experience' (Bombari, Schmid Mast & Bachmann, 2016, p. 63). PR's intervention in power brings a desirable unity to the power-holder's emotional experience: an intensely individual reward of power.

Why is this? It might satisfy the power-holder that communication control places the less powerful at an emotional disadvantage. It is harder for them to influence the power-holder's plans because they must pay more heed to the content:

Their dependency encourages them to attend to multiple cues in the environment, in search of any potentially useful information. Thus, they treat information more equally, attending not only to the central information, but also to the peripheral or distracting information.

(Slabu, Guinote & Wilkinson, 2013, p. 37)

On the other hand, strategic control of communication is emotionally satisfying for a power-holder for the opposite reason. A power-holder pays less attention to multiple cues, to adapting personal behaviour, or to interpreting the communication of less powerful individuals. Fewer cues can increase the tendency to use stereotypes as policy or a convenience, which 'all too easily result from power, from asymmetries in control' (Fiske, 1993, p. 621).

When people *do* have power, they *do not* seek complex information about others. Whereas powerlessness demands vigilance, power allows people to ignore the most informative cues about others.

(Fiske & Dépret, 1996, p. 34)

Stereotyping's asymmetry has communication value as a convenient shorthand. The identified stereotype can make individuals into the targets of a formulaic PR process from which it is hard to escape. It demonstrates the power-holders' reduced need to expend energy adapting their own communication to mirror others. It might be construed from this that the greater a power-holder's communication needs, the more extensive the mirroring disparity and the greater the gap between leader and led.

More satisfaction may also be gained by publicly showing that a power-holder or aspirant has less need to 'adapt and mirror' to others and more room to project a distinctive individuality. Machiavelli made much of this in *The Prince* (1513), including a chapter on 'How a Prince should conduct himself so as to gain renown' (Machiavelli et al., 1992, p. 102). Recommendations included the maxim 'liberality exercised in a way that does not bring you the reputation for it, injures you' (Machiavelli et al., 1992, p. 72); advice about the correct staging of events; public acts of justice and clemency; and praise for the distracting actions of the King of Spain who 'kept the minds of his people in suspense and admiration and occupied with the issue of them' (Machiavelli et al., 1992, p. 103).

The reward of less mimicry

Power-holders have less need to mimic others, and this is apparently experienced as a reward. Hogeveen et al.'s neurological study of power relationships highlights one possible part played by communication when it investigated 'how power is implemented in the brain' (Hogeveen et al., 2013, p. 755). They concentrated on the imitative qualities of the motor resonance system – 'the activation of similar brain networks when acting and when watching someone else act' (Hogeveen et al., 2013, p. 755). The results supported research that the more powerful the participants the less likely they were to resonate the actions of less powerful participants: 'high power leads to reduced processing of others' actions and emotions relative to low power' (Hogeveen et al., 2013, p. 759).

> One possibility is that the posterior superior temporal sulcus (pSTS), a brain region that sends visual input to resonant brain areas, is inhibited or somehow deactivated by high power.
>
> (Hogeveen et al., 2013, p. 759)

The reward of emotional dominance?

Projecting a distinct personality appears to be more powerful than imitating or interpreting someone else's personality. Why is this so? We must rely on hypotheses, although human history and science clearly demonstrate 'felt pride's' dependence on communication. 'The emotion of pride' in power-holding has been called 'a Darwinian adaptation serving to enhance social status through its rewarding effect on the individual' (Chapais, 2015, p. 162). It 'informs [power-holders] about their own value and merited status, and informs others about the individual' (Chapais, 2015, p. 162).

It is not quite speculation to ask if neuroscience points to the possibility, so well chronicled historically and philosophically, that a power imbalance rewards the power-holder with an emotional disparity between power-holder and the less powerful. The ventral striatum referred to earlier is influenced by 'emotional arousal exerted by a single interaction partner' (Klann-Delius et al., 2015, p. 442) and 'related to activity in bilateral anterior insula/IFG and DLPFC [brain areas respectively implicated *inter alia* in audio-visual integration activity and working memory, planning and decision-making]' (Klann-Delius et al., 2015, p. 442). The amygdala area of the brain is also linked to processing emotion (Morawetz, Alexandrowicz & Heekeren, 2016). Such a hypothesis might ask if these sources of emotional arousal are significantly activated; not just in one-on-one communication but in large-scale communication with subordinate groups. Zahn et al.'s paper on neurological proneness to pride and gratitude describes 'moral emotions' as 'blaming (guilt, indignation) or praising (pride, gratitude) themselves or others' (Zahn, Garrido, Moll & Grafman, 2014, p. 1676). Moral emotions must be aroused by communication relations between individuals, which may include individuals arranged hierarchically in organizations whether families, states, or non-government organizations. Zahn et al. imply this possibility by proposing a connection to 'social behaviour':

> Posterior cortical networks involved in visual imagery, although not necessary for moral sentiments, may play a supportive role in that they may allow for more lively and detailed scenic representations of social behaviour and hence more intense emotional experience when visuo-spatial memories or mental models are required.
>
> (Zahn et al., 2014, p. 1681)

'Moral-emotional' rewards of subordination could include the reward of pride. In which case it may be added that the experiment's 'non-predicted regional effects were that cuneus and precuneus volumes were reduced in pride-prone individuals' (Zahn et al., 2014, p. 1680). In other words, pride-prone individuals appeared to have less grey matter in two areas of the brain involved in several activities including self-reflection, reward expectation and some visual processing. Perhaps then, the nervous system of at least some individual power-holders is powerfully affected by the rewards of large-scale managed public communication. Perhaps PR helps an organization reach its leaders' objectives, and encourages responses from subordinated individuals which arouse neurological as well as material or political satisfactions among the power-holders.

PR, neuroscience and subordination

Why is the individual ready to submit to power? Is enjoyment of the pleasures of domination (borrowing from Xifra) matched by satisfactions of subordination? Humans may readily submit to power imbalances, like other species. Subordination and accompanying tasks must be continually reinforced, interpreted and justified, though, because 'the individual-group relationship is a part-whole relation unprecedented in nature, since it is the only part-whole relation in which the whole is represented in each part' (Fiske et al., 1996, p. 47). The communication advantages of subordination to the nervous system are not immediately obvious. It was noted above that subordinate individuals consume more energy interpreting power communication: decidedly not a reward. Are there rewards? Can communicated power offer more than material satisfactions to the subordinated?

Mimicry, desire, belonging

The neuroscience of imitation may help explain how desire to participate in the hierarchical tension between individuality and group can be aroused. Individuals often wish to mirror the values and behaviours of group power-holders. One of the mechanisms involved may be 'mirror neurons':

> A particular class of visuomotor[1] neurons in the brain that show activity both when an individual performs an action and when he observes another individual performing the same action.
>
> (Lacoste-Badie & Droulers, 2014, p. 195)

While visuomotor neurons are important, and may affect the brain's control over visual perception and imitation, care must be taken not to over-stress the 'mimicry' thesis as a reason for accepting power relationships or as an all-purpose explanation for mirror neurons themselves (Hickok, 2014). Power appears to consume more interpretive energy or imitation among the less powerful, but these acts of subordination can be connected to other factors.

Other explanations for the individual's desire to accept authority exist. Direct physical imitation interacts with several features implicated in individual nervous systems (Farmer, Carr, Svartdal, Winkielman & Hamilton, 2016). For example, power might be mimicked because it is neurologically trusted. High levels of trust, and even joy, have been linked with higher levels of the brain chemical oxytocin, which in rodents has been 'shown to signal that another animal was safe to approach' (Zak, 2017, p. 87). Trust may from time to time produce rewards for trusting a hierarchy. Reward stimuli stimulate neural systems responsible for incentive salience – 'a motivational property with "magnet-like" qualities' which confers 'desire' or 'wanting' (Zhang, Berridge, Tindell, Smoth & Aldridge, 2009, p. 1).

Cultural differences between responses to power also seem to reinforce the importance of communication, since power is expressed in culture and culture is a communicated quality. Rule et al. noted differing neural responses to communicated power:

> American participants exhibited significantly greater responses in mesolimbic reward regions (e.g., the head of the caudate nucleus) when viewing bodies posing dominance whereas Japanese participants exhibited similar activity when viewing bodies posing submission.
>
> (Rule, Freeman & Ambady, 2013, p. 4)

Communicating dominance and rewarding subordination exists in non-geographic cultures as well, created by values, pastimes, politics or purchasing decisions. In all these settings subordination may encourage areas of the brain implicated in mimicry, desire and belonging: rewards for accepting 'control deprivation as a function of group position in the social structure' (Fiske et al., 1996, p. 47), a point explored in Chapter 2. Following in the footsteps of Gustave Le Bon and other earlier students of the crowd, the '*psychological representation* of being part of a social group' if properly represented can outweigh the evolutionary disadvantages of independence from an organization's hierarchy (Fiske et al., 1996, p. 48). Individuals:

> Can be made happier if an ingroup has power, even if they personally have no control.
>
> (Fiske et al., 1996, p. 50)

Many questions about power, PR and individuality remain for neuroscience, which is starting to identify the individual's place in this interrelationship, and offering new ideas, new correctives. In *Human Action* (1949) the economist and philosopher Ludwig von Mises distinguished business power from the power exercised by states:

> It is very inexpedient to employ the same term 'power' in dealing with a firm's ability to supply the consumers with automobiles, shoes or margarine

better than others do and in referring to the strength of a government's armed forces to crush any resistance.

(von Mises, 1949/1966, p. 649)

This distinction is correct at the level of society, but it remains an open question whether the individual brain experiences 'felt power' in different ways from different organizations. Neuroscience is still in its relative infancy on this topic. So far it seems possible that individuality might respond in similar ways to communicated power by different human organizations, using the same areas of the brain. The only differences may be the media organizations use, and not inside the receiving mind itself. Might a face-to-face encounter with power differ from one communicated through a screen? History suggests that it may not be radically different. The historical deployment of increasingly sophisticated media to activate encounters between individuals and power-holders on a large-scale, flags a neural relationship that can be gratified by technology. There could be no subordinate relationship with power-holders without the rewards of desire, belonging and mimicry, situated in the individual brain and frequently engaged by managing public communication.

This is new light on older wisdom. Neuroscience is adding to the story of individuality, PR and power. It might eventually find a tipping point between individual self-ownership and part-ownership of our selves by any person, or group that communicates its authority. Like Machiavelli, Shakespeare well knew:

That no man is the lord of anything,
Though in and of him there be much consisting,
Till he communicate his parts to others.
    (Shakespeare, Troilus and Cressida, p. 733)

Conclusion

It is not power for power's sake but managed public communication that embodies power and subordination, and awakens rewards and desires within the individual brain. PR is not an agent of public power. PR is the face of a power, because power is socially and biologically experienced. Power is invisible without PR's 'invisible government'. In the public domain PR manages what Foucault calls 'the hazardous play of dominations' (Foucault et al., 1981, p. 148). In this way potential tensions between group and individual are managed. Because of this connection with power, PR's evolutionary effect on human individuality is old, deep and lasting.

The rest of this book is mainly about how the idea of individuality has changed with the evolution of a mind ever more amenable to PR, from origins described in these first chapters. The mind was to evolve alongside PR. How? The answer depends on what the mind really is, and if neuroscience alone can explain what happens to it when it is in contact with PR.

Note

1 'Visuomotor' describes anything related to the brain's ability to coordinate movement and visual perception.

References

Al-Farabi, N. & Walzer, R. (1985). *On the perfect state*. Oxford: Clarendon Press.

Arendt, H. (1994). *The origins of totalitarianism*. eBook. San Diego, CA: Harcourt, Inc.

Asch, S. E. (1951). Effects of group pressure on the modification and distortion of judgments. In H. Guetzkow (Ed.), *Groups, leadership and men* (pp. 177–190). Pittsburgh, PA: Carnegie Press.

Bault, N., Pelloux, B., Fahrenfort, J. J., Ridderinkhof, K. R., & van Winden, F. (2015). Neural dynamics of social tie formation in economic decision-making. *Social Cognitive & Affective Neuroscience*, *10*(6), 877–884. doi:10.1093/scan/nsu138.

Bernays, E. (1947). The engineering of consent. *The Annals of the American Academy*, *250*(1), 113–120. Retrieved from www.mcnuttphysics.com/uploads/2/3/6/9/23694535/engineering_of_consent-edward_l_bernays.pdf.

Bernays, E. L. (1961). *Crystallizing public opinion*. New York: Liveright Pub. Corp.

Bernays, E. L. (2005). *Propaganda*. New York: Ig.

Bombari, D., Schmid Mast, M., & Bachmann, M. (2017). Felt power explains the link between position power and experienced emotions. *Emotion*, *17*(1), 55–66.

Chapais, B. (2015). Competence and the evolutionary origins of status and power in humans. *Human Nature*, *26*(2), 161–183. doi:10.1007/s12110-015-9227-6.

Farmer, H., Carr, E. W., Svartdal, M., Winkielman, P., & Hamilton, A. C. (2016). Status and power do not modulate automatic imitation of intransitive hand movements. *PLOS One*, *11*(4), 1–31. doi:10.1371/journal.pone.0151835.

Fiske, S. T. (1993). Controlling other people: The impact of power on stereotyping. *American Psychologist*, *48*(6), 621–628. doi:10.1037/0003-066X.48.6.621.

Fiske, S. T., & Dépret, E. (1996). Control, interdependence and power: Understanding social cognition in its social context. *European Review of Social Psychology*, *7*(1), 31–61.

Foucault, M., & Bouchard, D. F. (1981). *Language, counter-memory, practice: Selected essays and interviews*. Transl. from the French by Donald F. Bouchard and Sherry Simon. Ithaca, NY: Cornell University Press.

Gandhi, M. K. (2008). *Autobiography: The story of my experiments with truth*. eBook. Thousand Oaks, CA: BN Publishing.

Guinote, A. (2007). Power affects basic cognition: Increased attentional inhibition and flexibility. *Journal of Experimental Social Psychology*, *43*, 685–697. doi:10.1016/j.jesp. 2006.06.008.

Hegel, G. W. F., & Nisbet, H. B. (2010). *Lectures on the philosophy of world history: Introduction: reason in history*. Cambridge: Cambridge University Press.

Hewlin, P. F., Dumas, T. L., & Burnett, M. F. (2017). To thine own self be true? Facades of conformity, values incongruence, and the moderating impact of leader integrity. *Academy of Management Journal*, *60*(1), 178–199. doi:10.5465/amj.2013.0404.

Hickok, G. (2014). *The myth of mirror neurons: The real neuroscience of communication and cognition*. New York: W. W. Norton and Company.

Hobbes, T. (2012). *Leviathan*. eBook. Oxford: Acheron Press.

Hogeveen, J., Inzlicht, M., & Obhi, S. S. (2014). Power changes how the brain responds to others. *Journal of Experimental Psychology: General*, *143*(2), 755–762.

Klann-Delius, G., Menninghaus, W., Prehn, K., Bajbouj, M., Korn, C. W., Jacobs, A. M., & Heekeren, H. R. (2015). The neural correlates of emotion alignment in social interaction. *Social Cognitive & Affective Neuroscience, 10*(3), 435–443.

Koerner, A. F., & Cvancara, K. E. (2002). The influence of conformity orientation on communication patterns in family conversations. *Journal of Family Communication, 2*(3), 133–152.

Lacoste-Badie, S., & Droulers, O. (2014). Advertising memory: The power of mirror neurons. *Journal of Neuroscience, Psychology, and Economics, 7*(4), 195–202. doi:10.1037/npe0000025.

Lippmann, W. (1997). *Public opinion*. New York: Free Press Paperbacks.

Lott, A. J., & Lott, B. E. (1961). Group cohesiveness, communication level, and conformity. *The Journal of Abnormal and Social Psychology, 62*(2), 408–412. doi:10.1037/h0041109.

Machiavelli, N., & Baker-Smith, D. (1992). *The prince*. New York: Knopf.

Madsen, D. (1985). A biochemical property relating to power seeking in humans. *American Political Science Review, 79*(2), 448–457.

Mandrik, C. A., Fern, E. F., & Bao, Y. (2005). Intergenerational influence: Roles of conformity to peers and communication effectiveness. *Psychology & Marketing, 22*(10), 813–832.

Marx, K. (1992). A contribution to the critique of Hegel's Philosophy of Right. In Marx, K., Colletti, L., Livingstone, R., & Benton, G. *Early Writings*. eBook. Harmondsworth, UK: Penguin Books in association with New Left Review.

Mill, J. S. (1977). On Liberty. In Edited by J. M. Robson. Introduction by A. Brady. *The collected works of John Stuart Mill*, Volume XVIII. Toronto: University of Toronto Press, London: Routledge and Kegan Paul. Retrieved from http://oll.libertyfund.org/?option=com_staticxt&staticfile=show.php%3Fcollection=46&Itemid=27.

von Mises, M. L. (1966). *Human action: A treatise on economics*. Chicago: H. Regnery Co.

Moore, E. S., Wilkie, W. L., & Lutz, R. J. (2002). Passing the torch: intergenerational influences as a source of brand equity. *Journal of Marketing, 66*(2), 17–37.

Morawetz, C., Alexandrowicz, R. W., & Heekeren, H. R. (2016). Successful emotion regulation is predicted by amygdala activity and aspects of personality: a latent variable approach. *Emotion*, doi:10.1037/emo0000215.

Nietzsche, F., & Samuel, H. B. (2003). *The genealogy of morals*. eBook. Mineola, NY: Dover.

Rousseau, J.-J., & Cranston, M. (2004). *The social contract*. London: Penguin.

Rule, N. O., Freeman, J. B., & Ambady, N. (2013). Culture in social neuroscience: A review. *Social Neuroscience, 8*(1), 3–10. doi:10.1080/17470919.2012.695293.

Schnuerch, R., & Gibbons, H. (2014). A review of neurocognitive mechanisms of social conformity. *Social Psychology, 45*(6), 466–478. doi:10.1027/1864-9335/a000213.

Shakespeare, W. (1988). Troilus and Cressida. In Shakespeare, W., *The complete works: Compact edition*. Oxford: Oxford University Press. 715–748.

Slabu, L., Guinote, A., & Wilkinson, D. (2013). How quickly can you detect it?. *Social Psychology, 44*(1): 37–41.

Stallen, M., & Sanfey, A. G. (2014). The neuroscience of social conformity: Implications for fundamental and applied research. *Frontiers in Neuroscience, 9*, 337–337.

Smith, P. K., Jostmann, N. B., Galinsky, A. D., & van Dijk, W. W. (2008). Lacking power impairs executive functions. *Psychological Science, 19*, 441–447. doi:10.1111/j.1467-9280.2008.02107.x.

Trotter, T. (1916). *Instincts of the herd in peace and war*. London: Fisher Unwin.

Vrecko, S. (2010). Neuroscience, power and culture: An introduction. *History of the Human Sciences, 23*(1), 1–10.

Wang, F., & Sun, X. (2015). Absolute power leads to absolute corruption? Impact of power on corruption depending on the concepts of power one holds. *European Journal of Social Psychology, 46*, 77–89.

Xifra, J. (2017). Reputation, symbolic capital and reputation in the seventeenth century: Thomas Hobbes and the origins of critical public relations historiography. *Public Relations Review*, http://dx.doi.org/10.1016/j.pubrev.2017.03.001.

Zahn, R., Garrido, G., Moll, J., & Grafman, J. (2014). Individual differences in posterior cortical volume correlate with proneness to pride and gratitude. *Social Cognitive and Affective Neuroscience, 9*(11), 1676–1683.

Zak, P. J. (2017). The neuroscience of trust. *Harvard Business Review, 95*(1), 84–90.

Zhang, J., Berridge, K. C., Tindell, A. J., Smoth, K. S., & Aldridge, J. W. (2009). A neural computational model of incentive salience. *PLOS Comput Biol, 5*(7), e1000437.

5 PR's future

Science and the mind

The last three chapters described some origins of PR's connection to individuality, PR's connection to the evolving inner life of the individual, and the ways PR affects the brain by using power relations. It is useful to consider if a PR-oriented science of the mind could change the way PR operates. This chapter asks where the mind as a whole intersects with PR, and if PR can capitalize on scientific knowledge and the older wisdom behind it.

It seems helpful to ask why our species' evolving complex mind is generally so open to fresh kinds of communication and especially the methods used in PR. It appears that PR, in ways not fully explained, satisfies the mind either as a biologically driven expression of the brain, or as something that to some extent acts independently of biology and ahead of signals organically generated by brain activity. PR may satisfy both these much discussed alternatives, but has not contributed to the discussion itself.

Then there is the act of creating meaning in the minds of individuals targeted by media and messages. PR knows roughly how to create meaning and achieve responses, but does not know why they work in the mind. If PR knew more about the mind, it could expand its methods, and increase its effect on the individual mind. More knowledge about complexity, the desire to be individual, the mind and mind–brain debate, the mind and meaning, and of cognitive science, could connect the science of the mind to PR's work.

The private mind and public complexity

Individual action in the public sphere is a response to the way information is communicated and interpreted. While the action might be, or feel, spontaneous, the information that caused it is not spontaneously generated. The noun 'spontaneity' is often produced to suggest authenticity, sincerity: the birth of a great truth from an allegedly un-doctored spasm of collective action. PR though is planned activity. What does science suggest about PR's ability to produce actions from audiences?

Much depends on understanding the mind's complexity. PR encounters complexity in individual reason and emotion, and when individuals contact groups; and it must lead the complex mind to complex behaviours. By managing this in

volume, PR changes or reinforces a given situation on an enormous scale measured by the impact on people in numbers and over time and geographical space.
Since the PR originators of this impact are often unknown to the receivers of
their activities, since the resulting complex changes can seem 'natural' rather
than planned, and since PR's route to the mind is about to alter with technology
changes it is timely to consider PR's connection with complex thinking.

Connections with complexity

Individual complexity is typically accompanied by escalating desire to supply or
receive information, and PR has flourished because of it. What aspects of
complex thinking matter, as far as PR is concerned?

One is the mind–brain issue just mentioned: whether the mind, particularly its
will and consciousness, is wholly an output of the material brain. This is determinate epiphenomenalism, often shortened to 'epiphenomenalism'. Or does the
mind have an indeterminate quality that can act independently or ahead of the
brain organism? Does PR affect mind complexity just by influencing the brain's
chemical and organic material, or are other influences involved? Another factor
is harnessing the areas of consciousness connecting private individuality to
public life via a 'collective unconsciousness' noted in Chapter 2. These are not
purely academic questions, although there is nothing wrong with that. The
answers, or the search for them, are already affecting the future and perhaps the
fate of PR, and of individual autonomy.

What is 'complexity', inasmuch as it affects the mind? First, it is of course
complex thinking, which enlarges human creative and reasoning faculties, which
then shapes the world individuality encounters. More complex thoughts produce
more complex societies. Functioning in them consumes more reflection from the
individual, generating more information, more communication, and more PR.

Second, complexity is relative, not absolute. It represents an advance compared with preceding moments. There is as yet no ultimate state to complex
thinking or societies; a society 'at rest' needing no further development may also
bring the evolution of managed public communication to a halt. Complexity is a
dynamic process, often needing renewal, using communication activities often
managed by PR.

Third, complexity is fragile. It spins an attenuated web of data compared to
the relatively more concentrated or confident simplicities that preceded it. Concentration of limited resources and limited communication often rewards simpler
organizations with more certainty and even durability. Then they are baffled by
changed conditions and cannot adapt. By contrast complexity's more extensive
social creations and the multiple activities needed to keep it in being increases
the vulnerabilities and potential rewards to organizations and individuals. For the
historian Joseph Tainter a reason why 'civilizations are fragile, impermanent
things' was their escalating investment in managing complexity to stay in being
(Tainter, 1988, p. 1). Complex organizations create more opportunities for strain
and tension. A sophisticated structure is no guarantee that all its members fully

conform to it. PR must often tackle the problem of reconciling complex societies, products or organizations with varying and sometimes-hostile individual needs.

Fourth, individuals and organizations may come and go but complexity overall has an evolutionary quality which necessarily escalates information exchange. It appears in the genetic life of plants and animals, as well as between and not only within humans, who can organize themselves, develop and apply technology, including communication technologies, to a greater extent than other organisms. In 1948 the mathematician Claude Shannon, working with Warren Weaver, proposed a (later adjusted by Shannon to 'The') 'Mathematical theory of communication' (Shannon, 1948). It has been described as 'the most versatile and fruitful concept of complexity' (Korb & Dorin, 2011, p. 330), and has been adopted in a number of disciplines. It established the idea of 'information-theoretic complexity' used by scholars of evolution, who continue to debate the principles guiding the length of the coded messages exchanged between complex systems.

Shannon's connection to PR is also well-known (*inter alia* Lee, 1993; Fawkes, 2004; Smith, 2012; Babiuk, 2015). Like evolutionary theory, PR captures much of Shannon's approach:

- Information source
- Transmitter: the interpreter of the information, who 'operates on the message in some way to produce a signal suitable for transmission over the channel'
- Channel: 'the medium used to transmit the signal'
- Receiver: who or which reconstructs or decodes 'the message from the signal'
- Destination: 'the person (or thing) for whom the message is intended'.

(Shannon, 1948, p. 7)

The mutual value of this theory to PR and biological evolution reinforces the possibility that PR affects individual complexity, indirectly by changing organizations and directly by changing the individual.

Finally, complexity is not entropy. PR's destructive powers cannot be linked to complexity. The act of undermining a competitor, rival or an entire social system with the help of managed public communication does not encourage complexity if destruction is the only result. An observation about evolution and entropy – the process of decline or decay in the natural world – should be repeated here:

Diversity (entropy) is not biological complexity, because biological complexity is specifically about adaptive, functional organization and not at all about thermal noise, accidental mutational load, or other physical disturbances.

(Korb & Dorin, 2011, p. 332)

PR's impact on individual complexity should be creative construction, sometimes achieved without entropy or possibly built on the wreckage of creative destruction. Destruction might involve complex communication but no complexity exists thereafter unless new forms rise from the rubble. Pitching entropic, destructive messages to individuals inflicts the same outcome on PR itself.

Assisting complex reasoning

PR encounters complexity with the division of labour into specializations described by Adam Smith in *Wealth of Nations*, unleashing the dynamic, sleepless, competitive forces described by Marx and Engels in the *Communist Manifesto*, leading to the 'process of creative destruction' and renewal described by Joseph Schumpeter in *Capitalism, Socialism and Democracy*, published in 1942 (Schumpeter, 2009, p. 81). Perennially innovative, accelerating, turbulent, discomfiting: individuality is not self-contained, and the division of labour ensures that it cannot escape the wider world. Paraphrasing John Donne: 'No mind is an island'. The British Moral Philosopher J. B. Baillie took the same position in introductory remarks to an edition of Hegel's *Phenomenology of Mind*:

> Individuality is itself only realised as a part of a concrete whole of individuals: its life is drawn from common life in and with others.
>
> (Hegel & Baillie, 1910, p. 429)

A continuous changing relationship with an organization's PR lets the individual inquire, solve and advance, and perpetuates separate identities for individual and organization, which need each other's distinctiveness. PR is the mortar that brings the two together yet keeps them apart. It is perhaps a subordinate and occasionally precarious position for individuality, but in this way PR is helping preserve individuality as desirable and distinct.

PR is used in this way so organizations can use individual complexity efficiently. Social complexity owes something to the ways managed public communication encourages dispassionate individual reasoning to make organizations more efficient. Complexity in organizations is often interpreted as a minimization of emotion, or feeling, and towards logic and reason. To stay on this path and achieve its objectives an organization continually seeks systems designed to divert individual contributions away from unhelpful subjects and onto improving efficiency.

Complexity inside organizations ideally if not in practice demands reason: foresight over impulsiveness, specialized skills over generic or general reflection, sophisticated information gathering and analysis over emotion, strategic direction of emotion over unpredictable emotion. The tiresome exhortations to be 'passionate' about a job are at root a disciplined strategic demand to pursue the organizational Will with more intense reasoning, because more reason is needed from individuality. Because of the rise of reasoning, PR must accommodate similar and symbolic forms of dispassionate complexity to ensure what sociologist Erving Goffman in 1974 notably called 'the organization of experience' (Goffman, 2010). PR must satisfy a characteristic in the individual that wants to build productive complexity and which is expressed by detailed knowledge and abstract reasoning.

The obstacles are well-known. For example, a detailed, 88-page Greenpeace scientific review of neonicotinoid pesticides and its accompanying PR encouraging social media conversations acknowledges a demand for dispassionate reasoning but tests the mental fortitude of target audiences (Greenpeace, 2017), and must partner with a more general publicity appeal to the senses. It is no coincidence that Tainter's diagnoses of advanced civilizations under strain is mirrored in individual thinking by a well-known information overload and the challenge of synthesizing it. It has been proposed that the incessant need to deal with information in business can cause an exhausted and overloaded individual brain to revert to less complex methods by a shorthand situated in the limbic system, associated with emotional behaviour and responses to memory:

> Judgment is impaired, and employees are left with only the ability to make decisions driven by emotion rather than higher-level rational cognitive thinking.
>
> (Buch, 2010, p. 45)

What has been aptly observed as 'the unity of the senses' in primate vocal communication 'converge on the idea that the neocortex is fundamentally multisensory' (Ghazanfar, 2012, p. 661) and passes information through this vivid filter for sensory experience implicated in 'higher order brain function', 'including cognition, sensory perception, and sophisticated motor control' (Lodato & Arlotta, 2015, p. 699). Human behaviour appears to be a non-uniform variant of the multisensory behaviours in primates, refined by important differences in environment and upbringing.

PR's interventions must overcome the mind's multisensory obstacles to reason and hostility to overload when rising organizational complexity demands more specialized actions from target audiences. The more complex the needs, the more individualized the PR becomes. One way PR may approach this problem with the technology soon to be available to it and discussed later in this chapter, may be by joining its communication more closely with what is often called the individual's continuous 'inner speech' which is 'also referred to as covert self-talk, verbal thinking, internal dialogue, inner voicing or self-verbalization' (Ren, Wang & Jarrold, 2016, p. 1). Initially developed in 1934 by the Soviet psychologist Lev Vygotsky (Vygotsky, 1934/1987): 'Recent empirical research has been largely supportive of Vygotskian claims about the functional significance of private speech, particularly its relations to task difficulty and task performance' (Alderson-Day & Fernyhough, 2015, p. 933). It is possible that PR's future attempts to intervene in public conversation require constructive impacts on private speech/inner voicing/self-verbalization. The findings of a 2017 study of inner speech (which it called 'verbal thinking') for people suffering Executive Function (EF) deficits are particularly suggestive for PR's advocacy of complexity:

> These results provide further evidence for specific links between verbal thinking and EF (particularly using multifactorial tasks of planning) and suggest that inner speech might serve as a key intervention target.
>
> (Wallace, Peng & Williams, 2017, p. 3456)

The mind's desire to be 'individual'

In complex societies individuality is a boon and an inconvenience to PR. The human mind's intensely, persistently and stubbornly individual features of consciousness and self-knowledge complicate PR's work. These features which currently cannot be definitively connected to 'mind–brain' determinism, seem most determined to make us feel our individuality, and individuality in other people and even things. The prominent philosopher and psychologist William James encapsulated the situation in a 1901 lecture 'Religion and Neurology', observing of 'things' that 'any object that is infinitely important to us and awakens our devotion feels to us also as if it must be *sui generis* and unique' (James, 1994, p. 11). Of our obstinate sense of individuality James added that possibly a crab might be outraged to hear itself disposed of as a crustacean: ' "I am no such thing," it would say; "I am MYSELF, MYSELF alone," ' (James, 1994, p. 12).

The collective and personal requirements of the mind are bound up in this self-knowledge and consciousness. One attempt to work with it is PR's cultivation of corporate 'personas' which Robert Reich calls an 'anthropomorphic fallacy' in *Supercapitalism* (Reich, 2007, p. 216); and which Burton Saint John III suggests could embody help for our dilemmas and hope for our aspirations, in *Public Relations and the Corporate Persona* (Saint John III, 2017). The dual public and private nature of the individual mind mean these interpretations are not contradictory. PR's application of the senses and reason to increase and direct human complexity will be advanced when the mind–brain's existence is finally confirmed or if the individual features of the mind are shown to be non-deterministic and 'essential to the very essence of personhood' (Clarke, 2014, p. 5).

Mind or mind–brain?

The question is important, maybe vital, to our understanding of the individual, society and their shared futures. PR's impact on the mind depends on the relationship between mind and brain, specifically between sensation and reaction. The Cartesian dualism noted in Chapter 2 is being challenged by the idea that the mind is affected by information biologically filtered through organs of the senses, ending with conclusions formed in specific areas of the brain. This is the idea of epiphenomenalism and the 'mind–brain' raised in this chapter. At the same time it is countered that: 'There is a kind of anomaly about the mental which is irreducible to the laws of nature' (Baber, 2013, p. 99).

If this view is correct, PR is something beyond a provider of suitable stimuli to prompt individual biology into action. Studying the neocortex and other areas of the nervous system or, say, tracking eye movements in response to words and images would not be enough to know the depth and complexity of the individuals PR seeks to engage. If the mind was more than an epiphenomenal bit of engineering it would also be possible for mental events to affect physical events, a reversal which could overturn or redefine epiphenomenalism.

To answer this problem some neurological research concentrates on the ways certain information is received, and by extension is communicated. PR would be revolutionized if the relationship of the nervous system to communicated power described in Chapter 4, for instance, involves something beyond the nervous system, something currently unknown, that PR is instinctively able to awaken.

Evidence for this 'something else' might lie in the individual's flexible sense of time, which PR frequently exploits. One neuroscientist observes that: 'While brain rhythms likely provide temporal metrics for information processing … they do not *a priori* provide a neural code for the conscious representation of time in the brain' (Wassenhove, 2017, p. 178). Understanding the conscious mind 'using the brain's internal time metrics' (Wassenhove, 2017, p. 177), might be useful to resolving the debate between mind and mind–brain. Insight may lie in understanding the order of events as they affect the individual, for: 'Unless it is shown that some physical events in the brain can be caused by some mental events, epiphenomenalism would be true' (Baber, 2013, p. 100).

If epiphenomenalism is the answer, 'the human brain might be more smart than it is complicated' (Churchland, 1993, p. 316). The complexities of the brain should in time be scientifically exposed and eventually directed. If it is confirmed that the mind is only a brew of neurons, dendrites, and signals 'defined broadly as the totality of those pieces of information' (Marlatt, 2014, p. 16), the business of communication, information management and perception forming would turn into a chemical challenge. PR would use neuroscience as a road map for sending client messages. It would concentrate on tapping the right parts of the brain, and perhaps in the end medicate with biochemistry to create mental events from physical interventions. If Cartesian dualism has no validity, PR's concentration on reaching – or treating – areas of a determinate mind–brain might even make large audiences unimportant, subtracting the 'public' from 'public relations' and substituting prescriptions for persuasion. In the end, PR might be replaced by a pseudo-medical procedure, a possibility touched on later in this chapter. Persuasion *en masse* would be redundant for what point would there be in laboriously distributing standardized messages to a group or attracting attention from group-directed media?

For these reasons, PR must know if individual consciousness can exist beyond epiphenomenalism and if, as a neuroscientist comments:

> The notion that some of our acts are the results of our willing them consciously is fundamental to how we understand selfhood and human relationships, love and hate, morality and responsibility, sin and repentance.
>
> (Clarke, 2014, p. 5)

Society too must know if PR works exclusively with a physical, material mind–brain, or taps non-material, or non-biological, conceptions that can connect to the organs of the senses and the brain.

At the moment PR exists to persuade, and persuasion assumes a degree of autonomy from the receiver of the message. PR might be able to offer evidence of non-biological individual autonomy. Can neuroscience suggest otherwise?

So far a workable compromise between an indeterminate consciousness and determinate (physically determined) epiphenomenalism has not been found. It is not enough to resort to the position of some neuroscientists, theologians, philosophers and psychologists that 'the neural activity underlying our conscious decision to act causes, or at least influences, the action' (Clarke, 2014, p. 8). If neural activity only 'influences' the conscious decision, the 'epi' prefix can no longer be applied to determinate (brain-originating) epiphenomenalism. What is the rest of the answer? Among other consequences the answer, if and when it comes, will decide how much PR may change, or stop existing.

While mind–brain neuroscience has been unable to confirm that consciousness sits inside the brain, several possibilities have been proposed but not conclusively proven at the time of writing. One identifies the brain's electromagnetic field (Pockett, 2011; Barrett, 2014; Hales, 2014; Liboff, 2016), finding it 'unlikely that any complex consciousness could exist in any field other than the electromagnetic field' (Barrett, 2014, p. 2). Consciousness has also been connected to fluctuating attention span in the brain's dorsolateral prefrontal cortex (Lau & Passingham, 2007; Bodovitz, 2008).

But if total epiphenomenalism is not the answer, then neuroscience can never find the key to individual consciousness, let alone how to influence individuality, because the whole answer simply will not be where it is looking. It would lie somewhere else. Where else? A danger for individuality may lie in arriving at a premature, mistaken answer, and applying it to manage information and perception between organizations and individuals. For instance the scientific spirit may rush society into mistaken conclusions about epiphenomenalism, determinism, and the mind–brain. It might – probably thanks to effective PR – reduce complex findings to non-specialists to dangerous simplicities and PR practitioners will act on them. Accessing 'mind–brain' consciousness with messages about what to buy, who to vote for, or which side of an issue is the most virtuous, may – almost certainly would if the wrong conclusions about the mind–brain are drawn – produce a crude facsimile of individuality. A behavioural 'Frankenstein effect' born out of misunderstood interventions inside the brain – could compromise that organ which may or may not hold the final answer to our consciousness and complexity, or PR's true place in it.

Mind and meaning

It was suggested earlier that PR affects complexity using emotion and reason and that this gives insight into PR's connection to the mind, to the epiphenomenal problem, and to the connection between PR and individuality. A brain is after all a medium, message and audience, and 'evolved to process factual information about the world' (Dunbar, 1998, p. 178). PR began as a natural response to the human's 'inherent tendency to make representations' which has led to communication activities that represent 'their inner worlds, the social world, the outside world, and the continuous and complex contact between these, in an infinite number of ways' (Sørensen et al., 2016, p. 21).

What remains is the 'hard problem of consciousness' which is 'the problem of *experience*' mentioned in Chapter 2 and identified by the philosopher David Chalmers (1995), among others. More specifically 'how any physical system, such as a brain, can give rise to subjective experience' (Faichney, 2013, p. 36). PR uses that experience to create meaning. Without meaning, an experience has no value to PR. Individuals largely create meaning by applying a blend of emotion and reasoning on the information they receive. PR is not always responsible for the information, but interpreting it is one reason why PR must combine emotion and reason, expressed in myths and symbols described earlier; or by the objective tone of publicity like that accompanying medical research sponsored by non-profits or healthcare corporations, aimed at expert audiences.

Knowing how the mind works to create meaning would revolutionize PR, but science has more problems than the arts deciphering and then codifying 'meaning'. Churchland's comment in 1993 is still accurate, just: 'The representational nature of thought has also appeared entirely beyond the capacity of a physical machine' (Churchland, 1993, p. 335). Of interest to PR is the connection between 'meaning' and emotions (also called 'affect' in neuroscience). Neuroscience is investigating it and sometimes starts with the propositions of Confucius, Plato, Freud, Jung and others in psychology, philosophy, religion and semiotics. According to one neuroscientist:

> Emotions are not just disturbances of the interior milieu, they also help control the way we perceive the world. As a corollary, we may need to consider that the ancient affective processes in the brain may have constituted the essential neural foundation for the adaptive creation of 'meaning' in brain evolution.
>
> (Panksepp, 2003, p. 9)

Is meaning created epiphenomenally by the mind–brain? Others support the view that emotion and meaning are united in the mind by information, and that 'emotion is the flavor of information and knowledge' (Sørensen et al., 2016, p. 33):

> We believe that there is an intricate relation between the categories of emotion, information, and knowledge, and that these concepts are the fundamental elements in the meaning creation process.
>
> (Sørensen et al., 2016, p. 22)

A version of the Shannon model appears to be reproducing itself in neuroscience to plot the connection between mind and meaning, especially since any meaning must be divined and communicated. There is for example more discussion about whether Language itself is genetically fixed. If that essential tool for communicating meaning is not genetically fixed, is it wholly learned within the brain, or is there an external element to our will to use language, and therefore to communicate the meaning we give it, and to either agree or disagree with others about how that meaning should be perceived?

Which comes first, when meaning is made in the individual mind? Is it an indeterminate understanding of knowledge communicated to us, or a determinate epiphenomenal processing of it? When PR creates meaning from its planned activities, is it conveyed by the knowledge and information already contained within that external activity or by a biological process in the brain? PR's work with symbols gives the impression that information must be externally managed and shaped to reach those areas of the mind to produce the response, which might contain varying degrees of feeling interleaved with reason. Are the organs of the senses and the brain capable of generating meaning without reference to any external source? Neuroscience has not answered this question. That will take scientific research that speaks more closely to PR's practical function.

Intervening in the mind: PR and cognitive science

Despite the enormous growth in neuroscience and its future possibilities for learning how to engage the mind, there is a large gap between it and PR that must be filled before the new knowledge can be applied. Meanwhile, the technical revolution makes answers imperative. PR has previously engaged the individual through groups, but social media means PR is paying more attention to peer power. It is using it to reach the individual mind often and directly, bypassing traditional news media and joining in conversations, as one leading practitioner put it, between '"horizontal" peer to peer trusted communications communities' preferred by the target audiences (Pickard, 2010, slide 21). Obstacles to this push towards engaging individuality include those imposed by traditional PR, by the media's own limitations, and by increased communication on more subjects by more organizations. New technologies try to keep pace by relaying, designing and interpreting complex information for business, brands, celebrities, states and nonprofits; creating new rules and opportunities for the management of perception by the management of messages. In such unfamiliar circumstances it might feel tempting to agree with the April 2017 headline of an ABC network affiliate in Utah – 'The Internet is eating your brain' by sousing the individual in Bernays-bequeathed propaganda (good4utah, 2017).

The results are well-known: 'Scant time for stories'; 'No attention span: distraction is a constant' (Pickard, 2010, slide 8). Those symptoms might be more prevalent among less specialized audiences or subjects. Audiences with specialist knowledge demand highly detailed information. Of course, an individual will be in either group at different times. The dual role invites reflection on how the mind works with information in different circumstances.

Given this, it is helpful to think about what PR can do with rational individual cognition; especially imperative when future media will include biotechnology.

Several organizations are trying to bring the brain and the internet into a closer relationship, and maybe complete harmony. Brain-internet and eye-internet interfaces are under investigation at Google, Intel, Elon Musk's Neuralink and the US Military's research arm DARPA, among others. Some initiatives are described later but today's breakthroughs will be broken through again tomorrow. One researcher and entrepreneur in this field has declared: 'Every time humans have contemplated the possibilities of a new technology, our imagination has failed us' (Claburn, 2017). PR's challenge is to its imagination, and whether it can learn from the people who first use the new tools. For instance, devices that may start as a boon for disadvantaged groups like the severely disabled will be adopted by others. Devices being planned today could give new scope to individuality by remaking the relationship between interior and exterior experience. It is inconceivable that PR will ignore the opportunities and problems a merging of mind and machine presents to its clients.

One response is to consult science research, especially neuroscience, and turn it into PR profit. The UK's *Observer* newspaper has rightly cautioned: 'The idea that the brain can reveal hidden truths about consumers is misleading' (Bell, 2015). It is wrong, to say the least, to see either new science or old wisdom as magical devices; MRI magicians conjuring profits simply by stimulating the right parts of the brain in the right way. It is another pathway to the Frankenstein effect. Few studies of the human mind so far have definitively filled the gap between scientific knowledge and PR's practice. PR still relies on 'intuition and creativity' in the words of the Chairman of Ogilvy PR, over science's 'huge body of emerging research in areas such as neuroscience, behavioural economics, social psychology and narrative theory' (Choudury, 2015). For the time being, precise knowledge is beyond PR. Many of its old approaches continue to work their own version of magic with the help of new media, social or otherwise, creating not computing ways to affect the mind over time and make it more complex without securing complete control.

A missing link may be cognitive science, which examines the mind as it reflects, perceives, makes decisions, navigates space and prompts the individual to action. Like PR, cognitive science is highly interdisciplinary and draws on neuroscience, psychology, philosophy, AI, anthropology and linguistics, among others. While PR and to some extent marketing have overlooked the field, it is a vital source of knowledge to User Experience Design (UX) which is the business of cementing relationships between audiences and organizations by the visual and content design of any device putting the two into contact. PR is starting to take an interest in UX itself, and related areas like content marketing and search engine optimization (SEO). Global PR giant Edelman for instance offers UX to clients as 'data visualization': 'Today's stories are complex. We help tell them through words and pictures' (Edelman, 2017). Another PR firm is committed to 'behavioral and cognitive science disciplines to deliver fact-based, results-focused campaigns' (Volume PR, 2017).

Gamification, machine learning and the brain–computer interface

If the mind is more directly accessible to PR in future, a next step is to investigate the cognitive research that guides UX, and apply it to emerging media of value to PR. Practical areas for study might for example include designing content optimally adjusted to the 'attention, planning, and working memory, time perception, and reward mechanisms' of particular target audiences. This was subject of a computer game study conducted with children by Peijnenborgh et al. (2016), and raises the possibilities of delivering messages more creatively. A connected possibility may be 'Gamification', 'the use of game elements in non game contexts' (Gatautis, Banyte, Piligrimiene, Vitkauskaite & Tarute, 2016), currently interesting to UX and some cognitive research for its potential to reduce disengagement and encourage cognition including memory, perception and action. Gamification's PR value could grow with every new generation of citizens, shoppers and employees:

> Individuals who have utilized some form of gaming technology throughout their lives may be increasingly comfortable in using game imagery to frame their organizational experiences.
>
> (Oravec, 2015, p. 69)

Machine learning will also have implications for PR's approach to individuality. Machines that learn from experience and generate their own algorithms without human intervention include text and face recognition devices. They will change the individual's connections to information and to organizations, as has every big change in media. Machine learning may mean that the human element in Shannon's model may matter less to organizations, but PR itself will exist as long as individuality must be invited to align with something; if not as employees or leaders, then through making choices between data the machines generate for them from purchasing decisions to social issues and ideologies. If individuality continues to matter PR must understand machine learning to inform machine advocacy, and influence machine dialogue, and perhaps to address public concern about the process. 'Machine to machine' (M2M?) PR is close but not quite viable at this point. 'Machine to individual' (M2I?) is already underway and referenced in Chapter 7, maybe followed by 'individual to machine' PR (I2M?) presumably for as long as machines need to learn from us.

Machine learning could create a deeper relationship between information and human user, which PR could not ignore. For all the mind's sophistication, machine learning challenges the brain's 100 billion neurons along with any indeterminate qualities the mind may also possess. PR would for instance apply cognitive science to tackle these challenges to human clarity and recall, and become an agent in the learning process. Failure to anticipate these changes – or ethically questionable PR – could once again drive the mind to a disproportionate reliance on sensory intuition when the task of absorbing new complex knowledge in new ways becomes too much. PR might use cognitive science to help solve this problem, acting as the 'we' in the recommendation that: 'By combining theories about cognitive psychology of learning and machine learning, we could make a completely new approach to decrease information overload' (Ketamo, 2011, p. 306).

The brain–computer interface (BCI) is a third area where PR is likely to connect with cognitive science to engage the mind. Currently, electrode implants in the brain are used to open neural pathways that operate prosthetics and help restore sight or movement. Other relevant applications include 'neurogaming' – controlling gamification directly via the mind, and direct brain-to-brain communication between human subjects which uses neurotechnologies and the internet to 'bypass the talking or typing part of internet and establish direct brain-to-brain communication between subjects located far away from each other in India and France' (Beth Israel, 2014; see also Rao et al., 2014). Is this the final fusion of media, mind and message? Maybe not, as theoretically 'cognitive-enhancing' drugs are already in use, including the nootropic class of drugs directed at motivation, creativity and memory which, effective or not, have enjoyed some publicity as a Silicon Valley favourite (Roose, 2015). The implications and temptations for PR will not be limited to helping cognitively impaired minds learn more, or cognitively alert minds work longer and better. BCI's chemically-assisted future for strategic communication needs caution but doubtless caution will be pressured by innovation, well publicized product claims, more sophisticated products able to dose audiences towards a PR goal and the individual's desire 'to trade health risks in return for cognitive benefits' (Mehlman, 2004, p. 487).

Cognitive-enhancing drugs might be developed to affect the mind in different ways, and 'enhance a particular type of intelligence while diminishing others' (Thaler, 2009, Commentary). Some PR practitioners will tout the time and money-saving possibilities of particular products for managing issues and crises, publicizing celebrities, launching products and building connections to communities or rather the individuals comprising them. All the more so since this media of cognitive-enhancing drugs can be widely distributed (and it will be media if it is not seen as media already, because a message is carried in it) (Butcher, 2003, p. 133). The impact would be intensely personal. This is not to say a message travelling on such a medium would work, if competing media and messages existed. It is possible some PR messages backed by drugs may prompt more individual introspection about the drugs themselves (Thaler, 2009), and the preferences of large numbers of users about the kinds of PR offered to them.

It is essential for PR to know more about the mind and the science revolutionizing our knowledge of the brain. PR practitioners must jettison some of their spontaneity and intuition – those supreme expressions of individuality – and rigorously pursue the scientific disciplines. For better or worse PR may need to remake itself using the science of the indeterminate or the epiphenomenal mind, of complex thinking, the mind and meaning, and cognition. It will create more complex relations and new levels of meaning between people, products, companies, brands, teams, ideas and governments. Last of all and true to the famous principle Bernays enunciated, PR would remain invisible.

Cognitive science appears in later chapters exploring how PR has intervened in the individual's life and the mind's evolution. One major intervention, and close partner to complexity, is the act of choosing. This is the subject of the next chapter.

References

Alderson-Day, B., & Fernyhough, C. (2015). Inner speech: Development, cognitive functions, phenomenology, and neurobiology. *Psychological Bulletin, 141*(5), 931–965. doi:10.1037/bul0000021.

Baber, Z. H. (2013). Consciousness of freedom and mind–brain identity. *Dialogue (1819–6462), 8*(1), 99–109.

Babiuk, C. (2015). Chapter 5. In L. A. Lymer, & W. W. Carney. (Eds.), *Fundamentals of public relations and marketing communications in Canada* (pp. 83–110). Edmonton, Canada: Pica Pica Press.

Barrett, A. B. (2014). An integration of integrated information theory with fundamental physics. *Frontiers in Psychology, 5*, 63. Retrieved from http://journal.frontiersin.org/article/10.3389/fpsyg.2014.00063/full.

Barton, C. (2014). Complexity, Social Complexity, and Modeling. *Journal Of Archaeological Method & Theory, 21*(2), 306–324. doi:10.1007/s10816-013-9187-2.

Bell, V. (2015, 28 July). The marketing industry has started using neuroscience, but the results are more glitter than gold. *Observer* (London).

Beth Israel Deaconess Medical Center. (2014, 3 September). Direct brain-to-brain communication demonstrated in human subjects. *ScienceDaily*. Retrieved from www.sciencedaily.com/releases/2014/09/140903105646.htm.

Bodovitz, S. (2008). The neural correlate of consciousness. *Journal of Theoretical Biology, 254*(3), 594–598.

Buch, K. (2010). Brain break: Understanding the influence of brain functions on organizational effectiveness. *T + D, 64*(5), 42–47.

Butcher, J. (2003). Cognitive enhancement raises ethical concerns. *Lancet, 362*(9378), 132.

Chalmers, D. J. (1995). Facing up to the problem of consciousness. *Journal of Consciousness Studies, 2*(3), 200–219. Retrieved from http://cogprints.org/316/1/consciousness.html.

Choudury, A. R. (2015, Jan. 24). The brainy communicator. *The Business Times Singapore*.

Churchland, P. S. (1993). *Neurophilosophy: Toward a unified science of the mind–brain.* Cambridge, MA: The MIT Press.

Claburn, T. (2017, 5 April). It's not just Elon building bridges to the brain: The Internet of Things is coming to a head. *The Register*. Retrieved from www.theregister.co.uk/2017/04/05/building_bridges_to_the_brain/.

Clarke, P. H. (2014). Neuroscientific and psychological attacks on the efficacy of conscious will. *Science & Christian Belief, 26*(1), 5–24.

Dunbar, R. I. (1998). The social brain hypothesis. *Brain, 9*(10), 178–190.

Edelman, P. R. (2017). Data visualization. Retrieved from www.edelman.com/expertise/data-visualization/.

Faichney, R. (2013). Mind, matter, meaning and information. *Triplec (Cognition, Communication, Cooperation): Open Access Journal for a Global Sustainable Information Society, 11*(1), 36–45.

Fawkes, J. (2004). Public relations and communication. In A. Theaker (Ed.), *The public relations handbook* (pp. 19–31). Abingdon, Oxon: Routledge.

Gatautis, R., Banyte, J., Piligrimiene, Z., Vitkauskaite, E., & Tarute, A. (2016). The Impact of Gamification on Consumer Brand Engagement. *Transformations in Business and Economics*, *15*(1), 173–191.

Ghazanfar, A. A. (2012). The unity of the senses for primate vocal communication. In M. M. Murray & M. T. Wallace. (Eds.) *The neural bases of multisensory processes* (pp. 653–662). Boca Raton, FL: CRC Press.

Goffman, E. (2010). *Frame analysis: An essay on the organization of experience.* Boston: Northeastern University Press.

good4utah. (2017, 25 April). The internet is eating your brain: Propaganda in the media. *Good4Utah.* Retrieved from www.good4utah.com/utah-wire/the-internet-is-eating-your-brain/699247520.

Greenpeace. (2017). The environmental risks of neonicotinoid pesticides: A review of the evidence post-2013. Retrieved from www.greenpeace.org/international/en/publications/Campaign-reports/Agriculture/The-Environmental-Risks-of-neonicotinoid-pesticides/.

Hales, C. G. (2014). The origins of the brain's endogenous electromagnetic field and its relationship to provision of consciousness. *Journal of Integrative Neuroscience*, *13*(2), 313–361. doi:10.1142/S0219635214400056

Hegel, G. W. F., & Baillie, J. B. (1910). *The phenomenology of mind: Vol. II/Transl. [from the German], with an introduction and notes, by J.B. Baillie.* (The phenomenology of mind.) London: Swan Sonnenschein.

Hoffecker, J. (2013). The Information Animal and the Super-brain. *Journal of Archaeological Method & Theory*, *20*(1), 18–41. doi:10.1007/s10816-011-9124-1.

James, W. (1994). *The varieties of religious experience: A study in human nature.* New York: Modern Library.

Ketamo, H. (2011). Managing information overload – Teachable media agents. In *Proceedings of the 8th International Conference on Intellectual Capital, Knowledge Management & Organisational Learning–ICICKM* (pp. 301–308).

Korb, K., & Dorin, A. (2011). Evolution unbound: releasing the arrow of complexity. *Biology & Philosophy*, *26*(3), 317–338. doi:10.1007/s10539-011-9254-6.

Lau, H. C., & Passingham, R. E. (2007). Unconscious activation of the cognitive control system in the human prefrontal cortex. *Journal of Neuroscience*, *27*(21), 5805–5811.

Lee, D. (1993). Developing effective communications. *University of Missouri Extension, CM109* Retrieved from *http://extension.missouri.edu/publications/DisplayPrinterFriendlyPub.aspx.*

Marlatt, L. (2014). The neuropsychology behind choice theory: Five basic needs. *International Journal of Choice Theory and Reality Therapy*, *34*(1), 16–21.

Liboff, A. R. (2016). Magnetic correlates in electromagnetic consciousness. *Electromagnetic Biology & Medicine*, *35*(3), 228–236. doi:10.3109/15368378.2015.1057641.

Lodato, S., & Arlotta, P. (2015). Generating neuronal diversity in the mammalian cerebral cortex. *Annual Review of Cell and Developmental Biology*, *31*699–720. doi:10.1146/annurev-cellbio-100814-125353.

Mehlman, M. J. (2004). Cognition-enhancing drugs. *The Milbank Quarterly*, *82*(3), 483–506. http://doi.org/10.1111/j.0887-378X.2004.00319.x.

Oravec, J. A. (2015). Gamification and multigamification in the workplace: Expanding the ludic dimensions of work and challenging the work/play dichotomy. *Cyberpsychology*, *9*(3), 59–71. doi:10.5817/CP2015-3-6.

Panksepp, J. (2003). At the interface of the affective, behavioral, and cognitive neurosciences: Decoding the emotional feelings of the brain. *Brain and Cognition*, *52*(1), 4–14.

Peijnenborgh, J. C., Hurks, P. P., Aldenkamp, A. P., van der Spek, E. D., Rauterberg, G., Vles, J. S., & Hendriksen, J. G. (2016). A Study on the validity of a computer-based game to assess cognitive processes, reward mechanisms, and time perception in children aged 4–8 years. *JMIR Serious Games, 4*(2), e15. doi:10.2196/games.5997.

Pickard, R. (2010). The persuasive storytellers: How the art of PR is becoming a science. [PowerPoint slides]. Retrieved from www.slideshare.net/bobpickard/how-the-art-of-pr-is-becoming-a-science.

Pockett, S. (2011). Initiation of intentional actions and the electromagnetic field theory of consciousness. *Humana Mente, 15*, 159–175. Retrieved from www.humanamente.eu/PDF/Issue15_Paper_Pockett.pdf.

Rao, R. P., Stocco, A., Bryan, M., Sarma, D., Youngquist, T. M., Wu, J., & Prat, C. S. (2014). A direct brain-to-brain interface in humans. *PLOS one, 9*(11), e111332.

Reich, R. B. (2007). *Supercapitalism: The transformation of business, democracy, and everyday life*. New York: Alfred A. Knopf.

Ren, X., Wang, T., & Jarrold, C. (2016). Individual differences in frequency of inner speech: Differential relations with cognitive and non-cognitive factors. *Frontiers in Psychology, (7)*. Article 1675, pp. 1–12.

Roose, K. (2015, 4 March). I tried Silicon Valley's favorite 'brain-enhancing' drugs. *Splinter News*. Retrieved from https://splinternews.com/i-tried-silicon-valleys-favorite-brain-enhancing-drugs-1793845948.

Saint John III, B. (2017). *Public relations and the corporate persona: The rise of the affinitive organization*. Abingdon, Oxon: Routledge.

Schumpeter, J. A. (2009). *Capitalism, socialism and democracy*. New York: Harperperennial.

Shannon, C. E. (1948). A mathematical theory of communication. *Bell System Technical Journal, 27*: 379–423 and 623–656. *Mathematical Reviews (MathSciNet): MR10, 133e*. Retrieved from http://lanethames.com/dataStore/ECE/InfoTheory/shannon.pdf.

Smith, R. D. (2012). *Becoming a public relations writer: A writing workbook for emerging and established media*. Abingdon, Oxon: Routledge.

Sørensen, B., Thellefsen, T., & Thellefsen, M. (2016). The meaning creation process, information, emotion, knowledge, two objects, and significance-effects: Some Peircean remarks. *Semiotica, 2016*(208), 21–33.

Suhay, E. (2015). Explaining Group Influence: The Role of Identity and Emotion in Political Conformity and Polarization. *Political Behavior, 37*(1), 221–251. doi:10.1007/s11109-014-9269-1.

Tainter, J. A. (1988). *The collapse of complex societies*. Cambridge: Cambridge University Press.

Thaler, D. S. (2009). Improving introspection to inform free will regarding the choice by healthy individuals to use or not use cognitive enhancing drugs. *Harm Reduction Journal, 6*(1), 10.

Volume PR. (2015). What we do. Retrieved from http://volumepr.com/what-we-do/

van Wassenhove, V. (2017). Time consciousness in a computational mind/brain. *Journal of Consciousness Studies, 24*(3–4), 177–202.

Vygotsky, L. S. (1934/1987). *Thinking and speech. The collected works of Lev Vygotsky* (Vol. 1). New York: Plenum Press.

Wallace, G. L., Peng, C. S., & Williams, D. (2017). Interfering with inner speech selectively disrupts problem solving and is linked with real-world executive functioning. *Journal of Speech, Language, and Hearing Research, 60*(12), 3456–3460.

6 Choice's infinite variety

Where choice meets PR

> In every case man retains the freedom and the possibility of deciding for
> or against the influence of his surroundings. Although he may seldom
> exert this freedom or utilize this opportunity to choose – it is open to him
> to do so.
>
> (Frankl, 1986, p. 98)

Choice's importance as a basic expression of individuality is well described by
concentration camp survivor and psychologist Victor Frankl. 'For or against' is
a personal choice, choice can be influenced, and PR must influence choices.
PR's frequent interventions in 'for' and 'against' decisions shape individuality.
If the 'opportunity to choose' is a gauge of personal freedom, then PR affects an
individual's choice by affecting freedom. How? What impact does PR have, not
just on a choice, but on the individual's capacity to choose freely? Is it too crude
to ask if PR offers genuine choice or an illusion of it, or are its interventions in
our 'for or against' moments more finely graded?

Choice, PR and freedom

It is hard to answer without understanding choice as a PR objective. Persuasion,
advocacy, dialogue in PR are means to the end of Choice. Choices are junctions
in the circuitry between organizations and individuals. A preferred choice must
be communicated and advocated by an organization, and the sum of individual
choices must be interpreted and folded into the organization's activities and
identity. PR intervenes when significant 'for and against' decisions are required
from key audiences. At any moment one action must be selected, one product
used over competing products. If choosing for and against things is a kind of
autonomy, then activities that support free choice are needed, and PR practitioners to manage their public communication.

 Milton Friedman is notable among those who believe choosing flourishes if
freedom is directly or indirectly encouraged by as many competing organizations
as possible since 'the greatest threat to human freedom is the concentration of

power' (Friedman & Friedman, 1990, p. 309). For PR, that principle is captured by the comment that 'what is truly vicious is not propaganda but a monopoly of it'. The words are credited to different sources, including a *New York Times* editorial in 1937, but with history's taste for irony they were spoken by the arch propaganda monopolist Napoleon (Holtman, 1950, p. i). Edward Bernays reproduced them in his 1952 historical and contemporary account *Public Relations*, written to show that PR evolved 'out of the needs of human beings for leadership and integration' (Bernays, 1980, Preface).

It is another irony that PR often perpetuates choices in favour of those looking to dominate their field, effectively encouraging a monopoly that discourages choice. The individual's ability to choose is not preserved by PR per se but by the fact that multiple choices naturally emerge in the PR rivalry of competing organizations. Victorious PR has strong incentives to close down alternatives, a tendency frequently apparent in public policy controversies. PR on the verge of defeat has an urgent and equal incentive to keep choice alive, at least until the tables are turned. Evidently choice opens a space to communicate stimulated by tension between at least two opposed forces, and the incomplete success of their PR.

Why PR must manage individual choice

Such freedoms and tensions matter but are not the foundation of the individual's wish to choose. To neuroscience it appears that 'decision making is a fundamental property of the entire nervous system that is present at nearly every stage of information processing ... in the sense of selecting one behaviour from a limited repertoire of alternatives' (Kalenscher, 2007, p. 26). It is studied and occasionally critiqued as a civic, political, legal, economic, biological, evolutionary, philosophical and rational phenomenon. Unsurprisingly, choice theory is a well-established cross-disciplinary subject. It is rarely examined in PR but given the role PR frequently plays in the choosing process it seems hard to ignore.

Analyses of choice are legion. At least three matter here. One is calibrating the balance between choice as a public and private action. Approaches to politics and economics are bound up with proposals for interfering, or intervening, in individual choices. Thus Plato's *Republic*, or Xenophon's fourth century BC account of the Persian state which described a system where the right of citizens 'to live however they please' was managed for 'the common good', so 'citizens will not in the first place even be such as to desire any vile or shameful deed' (Xenophon & Ambler, 2001, 1.2.2–3). In 1844 Marx attacked private choice as an exercise 'separated from the community as a member of civil society' (Marx, 1994, p. 17). He also criticized the political and civil problems of treating choice as an egoistic activity beyond society's control. In other words, personal choice requires intervention for the good of the community. We find a milder version of this view elsewhere, including a 2016 lecture 'Restoring rational choice', when the Harvard economist John Campbell suggested that 'household financial mistakes create a new rationale for intervention in the economy' (Campbell, 2016, p. 25). Is stronger external intervention in the act of choosing necessary or is it what PR does in any case, preserving individual autonomy at the same time?

A second connected area of inquiry is the influence of aesthetics on choosing. In PR 'aesthetics' include any factors encouraging a choice independent of the raw impartial data possessed by an organization. PR has conducted little scientific investigation on the aesthetics of its activities in deciding choices, although a bigger body of research examines the same subject in marketing. Research on food packaging does for instance find 'packaging design manipulations were effective in altering perceived healthiness and fat level while keeping expected tastiness constant' (Van der Laan, De Ridder, Viergever & Smeets, 2012, Behavioral results). The conclusion looks deceptively obvious. Consumer choices across a range of products are clearly influenced by shapes, colours, packaging or aesthetic suitability for the home (Bloch, 1995; Creusen & Schoormans, 2005). But the reasons for it are not obvious, most especially in PR. Why do aesthetics, the sizzle rather than the steak, affect choices in various PR activities like publicity, public affairs, or reputation, crisis and issues management? That they must do seems apparent, and also that they operate at a strongly individual level: 'Aesthetic responses are primarily emotional or feeling responses, and as such they are very personal' (Creusen & Schoormans, 2005, p. 65). Is this a learned response, or is there a connection to individuality through what has been called 'Darwinian aesthetics'? This is examined next using evolutionary theory, and appears later in ideas about 'intertemporal choice'.

A third area for inquiry is locating the roots of choice in the mind, which may illuminate how or why it can be influenced. Research on human evolution, for example, investigates the earliest impacts of choice on natural selection and diet, which enriches connected debates about whether habit gave rise to choice or vice versa, and the connection of choice to learned behaviour (Hodgson, 2010; Wood & Neal, 2007). One well-known place where habit and aesthetics meet is the high degree of personal ornamentation used in mate selection by many species first recorded in detail by Charles Darwin (Jones & Ratterman, 2009), more especially when the ornaments are viewed as media. It has been said of beauty standards in natural selection 'that it is not the content of the standards that show evidence of convergence – it is the rules or how we construct beauty ideals that have universalities across cultures' (Grammer, Fink, Muller & Thornhill, 2003, p. 385). If universal aesthetic rules guide selection, are they affecting the methods PR uses to influence the ostensibly 'very personal' aesthetics of individual choice, and if there are rules is the personal nature of that choice an illusion? Does a pair of sparkling eyes or an irresistible colour combination confuse or sharpen our complex, questing mind? Aesthetics, often viewed as a soft but necessary accessory by business, may contain hard truths about PR's impact on the choosing mind, on choice as a habitual or learned trait, and on PR's nature.

Choice matters to PR because it reinforces its messages with a sense of individual autonomy; revolves around the decision for or against something; must be communicated publicly; must be supported by communicating organizations to some degree; uses a nervous system that may work to universal rules about aesthetics; and joins an unresolved debate between habitual and learned choice. Lastly, PR's role in individual choice is part of a debate about what private choice owes to the public good, and presumably vice versa. It is a debate about ethics, or morality in choice. Is managing choice ethical, and how does it influence individuality?

Ethical and moral challenges of PR-mediated choice

Deliberate oversimplification

Choice is often explained 'as the maximization of value', which includes the practical utility of a decision (Shafir, Simonson & Tversky, 1993, p. 12). Such technocratic, reason-centred interpretations play a small part in what PR does with choice, strategically and morally. More important for PR is that simplifying the choice between for and against becomes essential to our relative and occasionally our absolute happiness. To choose something is to decide something with a measure of freedom. Choices are only made to obtain goals that choosers feel will benefit them materially, ideologically, emotionally or spiritually. The happiness achieved may be great or small; it may be misconceived; it may lead to unhappiness later on, but not at the moment of choosing. At that moment the individual opts for greater happiness relative to the lesser happiness believed to lie in the alternatives. In that short-lived and intense moment Kierkegaard's long, repetitive, celebrated, wry and wise remark about choice in *Either/Or* (1843) is neglected. Here is part of it:

> Laugh at the world's follies, you will regret it; weep over them, you will also regret it; if you laugh at the world's follies or if you weep over them, you will regret both; whether you laugh at the world's follies or you weep over them, you will regret both.
>   (Kierkegaard, Hannay & Eremita, 2004, Diapsalmata)

In other words, the long-term realities of any choice are forgotten in the 'rightness' of the moment. Perhaps this view assumes people philosophically contemplate their choice afterwards free from the noise of managed persuasion. This is a large assumption. Being persuaded to make that choice, and then being invited to continue believing in it, is what PR tries to do. For or against and their respective values can be continuously 'weaponised' by organizations to strip out ambiguity: reducing the act to 'for and against', and the choice to 'one or the other', not one or several others. Lenin was in no doubt about the need for propaganda to create binary situations for the chooser, and managing the communication process. Rooting out spontaneity, not as he put it 'bowing' to it: '*The only choice is*: either bourgeois or socialist ideology. There is no middle course' (Lenin et al., 1987, p. 82). Communism or Capitalism? Working class or bourgeois? Red or Blue? Liverpool or Everton? Coke or Pepsi? Reducing the number of choices (a familiar practice in public life) and perhaps converting them into universal symbols of large values creates an impression of simplicity, an urgency sharpened by imaginary space and time constraints, a conviction that the subject has been understood and reduced to its essentials. It is an attempt to harness individual morality by creating a definitive 'for and against', and a principle for deciding which is which.

Enforcing conformity

Nor can choices be avoided. Once presented, their messages exist in time. Kierkegaard again:

> It is a delusion to think one can keep one's personality blank, or that one can in any real sense arrest and interrupt personal life. The personality already has interest in the choice before one chooses, and if one postpones the choice the personality makes the choice unconsciously, or it is made by the dark powers within it.
>
> (Kierkegaard et al., 2004, Equilibrium between the Aesthetic)

Choice is unavoidable, which for PR gives it durability and communication value. Adam Smith approvingly described ancient Stoic opinions on these qualities of choice in *The Theory of Moral Sentiments* (1759): 'Virtue and the propriety of conduct consisted in choosing and rejecting all different objects and circumstances according as they were *by nature rendered* more or less the objects of choice or rejection' [author's italics] (Smith, 1759, Chapter 1, III Of those Systems which make Virtue consist in Propriety).

Choosing has a moral quality that reinforces its value to PR. First, to borrow from psychology, it contains 'valence': the chooser decides which option contains more 'goodness' and which more 'badness'. Second, PR weights individual choice with collective consequences. Apart from individual goodness or badness, the ideas about the morality of public and private choices raised by Marx and others are progenitors of the search for a morally watertight 'social choice theory', which includes 'the need to state explicitly what conditions must be satisfied by any social decision procedure to be acceptable' (Sen, 2012, p. 263).

But PR's use of social choice brings problems. Choice can be prompted in different ways. PR can present it in many compelling guises: as urgent or measured, casual or crucial, haptic or intellectual, impulsive or considered. All these methods share the condition that PR can use them to apply group pressure. PR often operates the machinery driving the 'tyranny of the majority' famously depicted in *On Liberty* (1859) by the philosopher J. S. Mill (Mill, 1977, Chapter 1). PR often promotes the idea that a decision has been reached by a group – that a commercially or civically useful target audience has made a choice into a truth, with the implication that anyone thinking otherwise is wrong in the face of the majority. A supposedly collective choice can be presented as strong and legitimate. 'Today', tweets a victorious French Deputy in June 2017, 'I would like to thank all the voters of the 2nd French constituency abroad for their trust' (Forteza, 2017).

Alternatively, individuals might use collective choices for moral and legal protection. Leaving its protection isolates and targets individuals like a former chief of the Indian Air Force, who defended himself against kickback charges in 2016 by describing the offending contract 'as a collective decision and was taken by the Prime Minister's Office but today they have thrust it upon me' (Siddiqui, 2016).

PR exploits perceptions that decisions are most valuable if they are shared by many individual decisions, mixing a collective morality into a choice which is hollow as pressure to conform overpowers the data behind the choice itself. Choice in PR is an encounter between the individual and the mass, adjusting the autonomies each possesses.

Exploiting negative emotions

If choice involves valence, it is open to the 'aesthetics' of feeling. Modern PR and its antecedents, not to mention the rhetoricians of the classical age or the poets of the Romantic era well knew that emotions 'generally facilitate decision making' (Gross, 1998, p. 273).

Science's interest is comparatively recent. Distilling choice into feeling also appears to simplify choice by 'limiting the amount of information an organism has to process' (Dickins, 2005, p. 375). This is scientific support for something PR has again long known and appeared earlier in this chapter. The moral impact of 'for or against', of persuasively simplifying or reducing choices for the mind to process shuts out or – currently a disturbing trend in civic communication – shouts down alternative choices by placing emotion over reason. Choice in the public arena is to some extent an expression of free communication which uses feelings and reason as a constructive aid to choice, and to another extent a feelings-driven distortion of the subject being communicated.

Individuality is not always a passive victim of distortion, however. An emotion-laden choice is likely to be affected by 'emotion regulation', when individuals 'attempt to achieve their emotion goals by trying to influence which emotions they experience, when they feel them, and how they experience them' (Markovitch, Netzer & Tamir, 2017, p. 728; see also Gross, 1998). It should be said that 'emotion' and 'mood' are treated here as aspects of the same underlying state of mind. The American Psychological Association has described mood as the 'pervasive and sustained "emotional climate,"' and emotions as 'fluctuating changes in emotional "weather"' (Gross, 1998, p. 273). Both are applied in PR to give the emotion-seeking individual a sense of a subject, alongside initiatives designed to create strong emotional spikes.

Negative emotions play a large part in this, and the individual is not a passive receptacle but can actively work with them if they are communicated. Some research finds that opposed choices do not need to generate opposed feelings: a 'good' choice does not need to arouse 'good' feelings. Investigation into the emotional influences on choice found negative emotions of fear and anger could be used to clarify a choice rather than to prompt negative reactions. They 'exerted unique influences on judgements – systematically shaping risk perception in a manner consistent with their underlying appraisal structures' (Lerner & Keltner, 2000, p. 484).

A 2015 study investigated the neural underpinnings of fear and the individual's management of it:

> The increased firing rates of the fear-responsive neurons indicate that consumers, when requested to enhance their emotions, can do so quite readily and successfully.
>
> (Cerf, Greenleaf, Meyvis & Morwitz, 2015, p. 542)

Beyond its 'contagious' qualities, fear may be managed and regulated by the brain to serve different purposes. How does this affect PR and choice? One theory, interesting for PR, pits the neural sources of negative emotions and rationality against one another to help individuals grasp the nature of the choice:

> There may be a competition on a cognitive level between neural networks representing the rational key to a problem with networks representing emotional heuristics. The winner of this competition inhibits the loser and dominates the decision, thus shifting decision makers between emotion and reason, fear and strength of mind, impatience and self-control, etc.
>
> (Kalenscher, 2007, pp. 26–27)

A façade for compulsion

Finally, in the hands of some organizations, particularly governments, choice may also be a façade for techniques that 'nudge' individuals from one choice and towards another supposed to be more socially ethical or profitable. The 'nudge' was proposed as a strategic option in 2009, with the goal of 'improving decisions about health, wealth and happiness' (Thaler & Sunstein, 2009), and taken up by governments, nonprofits and corporations. Early enthusiasts included British Prime Minister David Cameron, who established a 'Behavioural Insights Team (BIT)' known as the 'nudge unit' of behavioural economists and psychologists, and now independent of the government. Other UK government departments, and local and central governments elsewhere followed suit.

A nudge is not quite an order, and not quite persuasion. A diluted version of choice is often offered with the preferred choice implied, or nudged forward, by the presiding organization. 'We use the term "nudging"' wrote the authors of a Toronto University report on the subject 'to mean a deliberate change in choice architecture with the goal of engineering a particular outcome' (Ly, Mazar, Zhao & Soman, 2013, p. 6). At its worse, suggests one scholarly observer, nudging 'undermines our autonomy and raises the cost of perfectly rational behavior that government planners simply fail to make sense of' (Anomaly, 2013, p. 304). Well-meaning examples include Copenhagen's use of spatial navigation unconsciously nudging people to deposit litter (Ly et al., 2013, p. 10); or as one fitness company did, launching 'motivational fees' where: 'Participants set a target number of gym visits each week and need to pay a penalty fee when they miss a gym session' (Ly et al., 2013, p. 12).

An academic co-author of the Toronto University report said: 'We stay away from any restrictions. Nudging isn't about banning stuff. Nudging is about giving people the freedom of choice, but steering their choice' (Lu, 2013). Well-meaning or not, 'steering their choice' is no choice at all. The real chooser is the organization, not the individual. 'Engineering a particular outcome' is a façade for an instruction, and nudging is a simulacrum of PR made to obtain a result without the effort of persuasion or dialogue. Nudging is not what *PR Week* once enthusiastically headlined as: 'A nudge and a think' (Maule, 2015). When is a nudge a gentle push or sharp elbow? The co-author of the 2009 bestseller *Nudge*, a behavioural economist, later defended the technique in PR fashion by focusing on the nomenclature and calling it a 'prompted choice', not a 'mandated choice' (Thaler, 2016, p. 329). Prompted or not, a choice without dialogue or persuasion is no choice. It is truly 'engineering' consent and lifts a veil on future PR's darker neuroscientific possibilities. Nudges mandate the group above the individual, who like a laboratory creature is steered with behavioural prompts. Utilitarian claims about achieving the greatest happiness of the greatest number forget that the greatest number does not necessarily produce the greatest individual happiness.

PR needs autonomous individual choice to exist, if it is to persuade or build dialogue. It is currently an actor in a more even communication relationship between organizations and individuals than is advertising, or unadulterated propaganda. Choices have a richer news value that instructions or nudges do not. Instructions do not need to use news-focused media platforms at all, except as pretence or simply for issuing orders.

Of course pretences and other sleights of hand are used in nudge-free PR. Misleading promises of relatively greater happiness might be implied or made. We have also seen that PR might reduce choice to a binary 'for and against', when a more nuanced series of options could be more truthful and helpful for the individual. We have seen that choices must be used in PR, and at least interpreted by PR because the individual cannot help making them. Choice is crucial to human consciousness and will, which are vulnerable to compelling depictions of a collective will that does not really exist.

PR knows choices often need emotional embellishments to override the logic of an alternative. Its problematic techniques include designing overpowering emotional aesthetics to push a preferred choice. It can imply unanimity and relative happiness on utilitarian grounds, and exploit the individual's ability to apply negative feelings to the decision process. All these methods create the sense of an autonomous decision, but not the reality. Do such methods enlarge our sense of self or undermine it completely? Reverting to Frankl, does PR truly present an individual with the possibility of freely 'deciding for or against the influence of his surroundings' (Frankl, 1986, p. 98)? Or does individuality collaborate in its own subjection? Does more choice mean more ownership over our selves: more 'self-ownership', or the reverse in the hands of PR? Is PR's work with choice weighed in the balance and found wanting? PR needs choice as a technique. Does choice need PR? Would individuality be stronger without PR-mediated choice, or are there advantages to the connection? To ask if PR's use of choice might strengthen individuality is to ask how the individual decides, and what PR does to that process.

The moment of choosing and what PR does

Choice is bound into the nervous system. 'We choose all our actions and thoughts and, indirectly, almost all our feelings and much of our physiology' (Glasser, 1998, p. 4). If PR wants to understand its impact on individuality at the moment of choosing, neuroscience and other sciences have a contribution to make.

Acknowledging individual autonomy

If individuality exists it must possess the autonomy outlined in Chapter 2 and by Frankl at the beginning of this chapter; an inner core equipped to decide without necessarily submitting to external stimuli, including PR's arts and science of persuasion. But is Frankl right? Or is the characteristic he describes too fragile to protect autonomous choice from PR? It is not encouraging to read about experiments on deliberately trapped rats, whose brains have useful resemblances to human brains (if neuroscientists want to learn about humans, they frequently turn to the rat for guidance). After a period of entrapment accompanied by electric shocks, the rats did not try to escape when the opportunity was finally presented to them (Hajszan et al., 2009). Evidently, a choice could be undermined by 'learned helplessness' in a rat (Hajszan et al., 2009, p. 392 *passim*).

Is it the same for humans? History offers many discouraging cases of individuals and entire societies cooperating in their own subjection even when alternatives presented themselves. A slightly more encouraging hypothesis suggests that restrictions on free choice actually confirm its importance:

> There is support for freedom as a basic need based on the conclusion that if individuals are unable to meet their need for freedom changes in certain brain structures, particularly the hippocampus, will result in functional deficits.
>
> (Marlatt, 2014, p. 18)

The possibilities for choosing can be studied as 'intertemporal choice' – choosing one course of action or reflection over another at different moments of time. Intertemporality influences PR's approaches to past, present and future to shape our perception at the moment of choosing. Perhaps it is more fundamental to PR's existence than its need to persuade or encourage dialogue. PR must prepare individuals for a moment that is, or feels, freely reached by marshalling messages and activities using time as an asset. If time was not a potential asset, PR would not need to appeal to memory and its impact on individuality would be less profound.

PR's connection to moment and memory is affected by the Information Revolution's impact on decision-making. A sign of this is the growth of 'conversation' – centred PR to build more personal and long-term relations with target audiences. According to Richard Edelman of the multinational Edelman PR: 'it is conversation – direct genuine interaction – with corporations that people want, not one way selling' (Edelman, 2011). Conversation-based PR is not a transient development. It responds to that growing and well-recorded individual sense of autonomy – be it real or imaginary – which digital media is unlocking.

Conversation-based PR might be used when organizations need to delay choices from target audiences who may prefer a quicker decision. 'Discounting of delayed rewards', one researcher notes:

> Refers to the observation that the value of a delayed reward is discounted (reduced in value or considered to be worth less) compared to the value of an immediate reward.
>
> (Takahashi, 2005, p. 691)

An intricate issue, a clear organizational identity, a complex product or a familiar brand cannot always trust sudden decisions from a target audience disinclined to treat patience as a virtue. For this reason conversational PR must be approached differently to a traditional campaign 'sprint':

> It's a marathon. It's a bit like dating. If you start a relationship with someone today, call them every day for a few weeks and then go silent, don't expect them to be thrilled to see you when you show up a year later.
>
> (Falkow, 2016)

Freeing choice from the trap of linearity

However, PR must sometimes prompt an immediate choice by creating a powerful mental desire for it: an offer of jam today rather than tomorrow, to use *Alice Through the Looking Glass*. In that case, feeling is an ally. PR obeys a nineteenth century 'law' formulated by the psychologists, physicists and philosophers Ernst Weber and Gustav Fechner. They had proposed 'that the external stimulus (e.g. loudness) is scaled into a logarithmic internal representation of sensation (Weber's law), rather than a linear internal representation' (Takahashi, 2005, p. 692). PR is able to rearrange linear representations to stimulate sensation even under time pressure, enriching perspectives by interfering with chronology, embodying McLuhan's 1964 observation that 'concern with effect rather than meaning is a basic change of our electric time' because 'effect involves the total situation, and not a single level of information movement' (McLuhan et al.,

2013, Chapter 2). This process is invigorated as PR turns to social media, which currently bridges the gap between traditional media and the biomedia to come. For instance, a crisis-hit organization seeking trust from key publics, and its opponents seeking the same objective, might both disorder time by creating a social media 'legacy' that need not be viewed, heard or read in order and indeed rarely is during and after the crisis. To influence choices, PR uses new media to disturb traditional ordering of events in time, and jumble chronological patterns to influence a choice.

Examples of this include the 2008 Canadian listeriosis outbreak linked to two slicing machines at a Maple Leaf Food plant in Toronto, which caused 22 deaths and 35 non-fatal injuries. The company embarked on a successful crisis communication plan with four important themes to signal the transition from reaction to recovery: 'product safety, Government investigation, corporate reputation and product reputation' (Howell & Miller, 2010, p. 49). But this customary temporal ordering was, as in other crises, complemented by other uses of time to shape decisions about the company's credibility. Social media ensured that the crisis does not have to be viewed in temporal order. The initial apology as the tragedy struck, the recovery process and the move to taking ownership of the food safety issue could be visited on YouTube and not in the order of the events themselves. Interested parties can still choose the valence of what happened long after the event, retrieving 'before than' and 'later than' activities in no particular order.

Social media can influence perceptions and decisions by escaping the one-way limitations of 'time's arrow' and rearranging chronologies to drive choices (YouTube, 2017). SEO is enhancing the possibilities of this 'non-chronological' approach for all kinds of PR, which is capable of managing such temporal rearrangements. In certain circumstances they parallel the rearrangements that may trigger drug dependent patients' loss of self-control, disarranging our standard perception of the temporal process, and often producing discomfort and disorientation. This is damaging for drug victims but potentially constructive for the audiences PR may target. It invites them to decide without confining their views inside a single order of events, and offers alternative temporal arrangements to inform their choice.

Respecting subjectivity

PR works closely with time in the individual's subjective sphere to generate choices. An unwelcome intrusion on the face of it. Subjectivity can frustrate purely objective decision-making that tries to protect reason from emotion, and consequently any blandishments from the persuaders. This approach to choice suggests that: 'the objective intensity of a stimulus is distinct from the subjective intensity that guides behavior' (Kable & Glimcher, 2007, p. 1625). Can objectivity really be divided from subjectivity in this way? Or is there a subjective quality to the mind–brain that is also 'encoded in the brain' (Kable et al., 2007, p. 1625), perhaps implicated in at least one area and common to anyone making a choice? Neural subjectivity, if it exists, must be respected if individuality is respected.

Much neuroscience research plots neural responses to objective elements in choice but by measuring neural activity using functional magnetic resonance imaging (fMRI), the psychologist Joseph Kable and neuroscientist Paul Glimcher sought neural responses to subjective choices by investigating delayed and immediate rewards. It is interesting that activity was recorded in the same areas of the brain that are active in communicated power relations (see Chapter 4). This by no means proves any neural connection between power and choice, yet. Nevertheless:

> Activity in parts of the ventral striatum, medial prefrontal cortex and posterior cingulate cortex were correlated with subjective value in each subject.... These same regions thus exhibited a different pattern of activity across subjects, with each subject's idiosyncratic pattern of brain activity being predicted by that subject's idiosyncratic preferences.
>
> (Kable et al., 2007, pp. 1628–1629)

Neural activity in these three areas:

> Tracks the subjective value of rewards as determined from behavior, rather than tracking a theoretically defined component of value that is more impulsive ... or more patient ... than the person's behavior.
>
> (Kable et al., 2007, p. 1630)

This, concluded the authors: 'provides unambiguous evidence that the subjective value of potential rewards is explicitly represented in the human brain' (Kable et al., 2007, p. 1625). In other words, subjectivity is not random, not an outlier, not an unnecessary and deceitful distraction. It is as integral to individuality as objectivity and a necessary actor in choosing. It may be identified as a neural activity, is therefore amenable to communication, and cannot be fully suppressed in favour of unalloyed objectivity. It is there to be used and Choice tells PR that it *must* use subjectivity. Choice may reveal that PR, by understanding the neural paths to subjectivity, can enrich its work and should not trust all its future development to a science of 'objective' communication. Choice as a subjective neurally embedded act opens the individual mind to the imaginative and aesthetic potential of strategically managed communication. The possibility is supported by Glimcher and Kable's work with neuroscientist Kenway Louie, again on the neural activity implicated when choosing between delayed versus immediate gratification:

> We found that rather than being simply impulsive, as has been previously supposed, our choosers seemed to adopt an 'as soon as possible' rule. The soonest possible gains were preferred at a more than exponential rate.
>
> (Glimcher, Kable & Louie, 2007, p. 146)

Neuroscience may be showing that by arousing subjectivity PR is not exploiting deceiving impulses but working with something vital to individuality even when it urges the mind towards impatience and immediate gratification, rather than to the prudence and more limited neural activity associated with delay. Delay, prudence, restraint in the process of choosing, cutting free from some of the immediate pressures of intertemporality: these might need a different approach – perhaps more measured and conversational – that could be harder to enrich with subjective PR.

Satisfying valuing and value

A good deal of research necessarily seeks to understand PR's value to the economy, or how it might be organized: 'to provide the greatest value to organizations, publics, and society' (Grunig, 2006, p. 153). PR also influences *perceptions of value*; it must evoke a value to encourage publics towards its desired choice. Neuroeconomics explores the neural process behind 'value coding': assigning a value to objects and its impact on a decision. One recent study 'finds overlapping signals of value coding in two brain regions central to the valuation process: the ventromedial prefrontal cortex and the ventral striatum' (Stott & Redish, 2015, p. 1). A related investigation of economic decision-making also reported overlaps in regions of the brain, suggesting that: 'the function of the striatum in human decision-making may overlap more with that of the cortex than previously thought' (Strait, Sleezer & Hayden, 2015, Discussion).

Stott and Redish ask what value actually is. They point out that 'multiple representations of value' have been suggested. If there is no one unifying concept: 'We come to an interesting question of arbitration and mediation and what drives behavior in these conflict situations' (Stott et al., 2015, p. 5). PR may be external evidence that value does not have a single core concept within the mind. It seems possible that PR assists in the arbitration and mediation of value coding, not merely numerical value, but of course overall value which includes abstract value and the value of personal reward from the choice, culminating in the choice itself. PR frequently asks individuals to choose representations of value on behalf of those it represents. Such choices do often need exterior influences and data but once again the moment of decision is an individual one. PR is therefore an activity that must respect the individual's power to agree or disagree with the proffered value, even as it aligns the value with the purported identity of a larger group the individual might feel part of.

It is relevant to value coding and PR to consult the distinctions often made between episodic, value and memory-based decisions – the first based on specific episodes from the past, the second on the personal advantages or 'subjective value' of the options presented to the individual, the third retrieving memories of connected likes or dislikes to reach a decision in the present (Weilbächer & Gluth, 2016, pp. 1–2). Recent research points to a strong relationship between the hippocampus (HPC) dominated brain activity connected with episodic memory, and the ventromedial prefrontal cortex (vmPFC) activity crucial to value-based decisions.

Dynamic Causal Modeling (DCM) of the fMRI data, a technique that allows measuring the extent and direction of effective connectivity between distant brain regions, revealed that the coupling from HPC to vmPFC was not only important for processing memory-based decisions in general but also for mediating the memory bias.

(Weilbächer et al., 2016, pp. 1–2)

Hard definitions of choice as episodic, value-focused and memory-based may in fact be blurred by collaboration between different regions of the brain when it assigns a PR-mediated value to a choice, adulterating (as we have already seen) the firm category of rational decision-making by seeming 'to encode the subjective values of different types of rewards on a common scale' with 'a neural common currency for choice' (Levy & Glimcher, 2012, p. 1027).

PR can deeply influence the individual mind at the moment of decision. How it does this looks obvious, but it is not, nor has it been explored. The knowledge explosion in neuroscience, in biotechnology, and related disciplines demand that PR understand its contacts with the individual more deeply at the moment of decision. That moment is when its influence with the individual and for the organization is decided. Paraphrasing an earlier observation about decision-making, PR is an arbiter and mediator, attempting to drive individual behaviour when a choice must be made. It must successfully imprint a value and create a compelling tension between desire and time that urges the chooser to the choice.

Choice is further evidence that PR exists because individuals must first feel persuaded if they are to be led to choose, at least to start with. Choice is undoubtedly a time for PR to wield its power; it is also a relationship in which the appeal to the individual must bring the brain's subjective and objective decision-making areas into constructive collaboration, as it does with emotion and reason. This applies to all managed public communication, including the propaganda activities of totalitarian states. Even there, pretensions to persuade and converse must be made, often using mass spectacle. Even in such states communication must show sensitivity to the human aspiration to choose, or pretend to.

If PR's place in society and its future effectiveness is to be gauged, if products are to sell, pipelines installed or resisted, celebrities embraced or repulsed, we must know more about PR's neurological part in promoting choices. In future, individuals will be engaged more directly, more vividly, less publicly and more personally when asked to choose. It is possible that a 'free media' will matter less than a 'free mind' or 'free expression' generally because the media in its current form, already being upended by social media, will be gone. Social media could itself be gone, part of a transition to brain-to-brain or other forms of neural media directly accessing the mind. If audience identities continue to have a value to PR, and to decision-making, it will involve an individual identity enhanced by the media of the mind introduced in Chapter 5, and discussed in the next chapters.

PR enriches individual choice – for now

An attempt must be made to answer the questions raised at the start of the chapter. Traditional PR makes choice a public matter: lifting it from an individual's private sphere into public experience. We can say that the individual mind demands that PR make its publicized choice as personal as possible, conflating aesthetics, data, moralities, time, complexity and simplification to stimulate cooperation from opposed areas of the brain. The philosopher George Santayana suggested in 1923 that for 'knowing' to occur, physical 'substance' – events in time – by itself is not enough. There must be 'belief in substance' based on experience stimulated by memory (Santanyana, 1990, p. 233). The observation is fitting for PR. To obtain a choice, PR has the moral duty of translating physical substance into believable personal experience, into feeling and memory, and accept any risks that come when a mere choice turns into a hard truth.

Beneath all this is the point raised at the start of the chapter; that persuasion or dialogue is less important to PR than choice. There has been much discussion in PR research about PR's role in persuasion, and in promoting an even dialogue between audiences and organizations. A debate over seeing PR as persuader or dialogue-agent is long-standing (see Pfau & Wan, 2006). It has been suggested here that both are means to the practical end of encouraging a choice, and potentially disposable if more effective methods appear. This could happen soon. For future practitioners, and perhaps for scholarship as well, a more direct, competitively attractive, path to securing a choice from individuals will probably require knowing the neuroscience behind choice and how new media lets PR reach human or unhuman minds more directly. It raises questions about what that kind of PR could do for, with and to individuality. For now, it can be said that competitive PR largely enriches not erodes the individual's capacity to choose freely on a range of subjects, largely because PR is imperfect, as imperfect as the people and data it must work with, and must to some extent try to talk to and with the individual. As an art PR must remain open to surprise flashes of subjective creativity. It is ironic that this creative component in PR, this guarantee that persuasion or dialogue matters, may not be used in future ahead of scientific knowledge about the brain's processing of choice. A double irony is that more effective media for publicizing choices are coming which provide moments of imagination so convincing that receptive individuals will not want to consider rival persuasions or dialogues, at least in the epiphenomenal portion of the mind.

In many societies organizations value the individual desire and ability to choose which is evolutionary, neurally embedded, habitual and possibly spiritually invigorating. If the idea of choice no longer served a competitive purpose and organizations were active users of biomedia, PR would then become public instruction. Debates about persuasion and dialogue in PR would end because all three will be redundant except as empty gestures in the direction of a vanishing time. Persuasion and dialogue would be replaced, at best by the wholesale use of the 'nudge', at worst by outright propaganda. Choice keeps organizations and

PR comparatively honest; competitive PR helps keep choice comparatively honest, but the individual must continue to want choice as a technique for reaching decisions in managed public communication.

What the end of persuasion or dialogue means for all that and for individuality itself is an open question. So far, an order is not PR. To choose freely between different persuasions or dialogues shows that the individual has a degree of ethical independence (Hove & Paek, 2017) that acts in the mind at the moment of decision, and that PR must recognize. The end of this book asks about the future prospects for this interaction in 'for or against' PR and for other aspects of individuality affected by PR. It is not an idle inquiry. Accelerating changes in science and technology demand that the problem is considered more widely, and now.

References

Anomaly, J. (2013). The manipulation of choice: Ethics and libertarian paternalism. *Independent Review*, *18*(2), 301–305.

Bernays, E. L. (1980). *Public relations*. eBook. Norman, OK: University of Oklahoma Press.

Bilgrami, A. (2016). Failures of Mind and Meaning. *Social Research*, *83*(3), 549–571.

BIT. (2017). Behavioural Insights Team. Homepage. Retrieved from www.gov.uk/government/organisations/behavioural-insights-team.

Bloch, P. H. (1995). Seeking the ideal form: Product design and consumer response. *The Journal of Marketing*, *59*(3), 16–29

Campbell, J. Y. (2016). Richard T. Ely lecture: Restoring rational choice: The challenge of consumer financial regulation. *American Economic Review*, *106*(5), 1–30. doi:http://dx.doi.org/10.1257/aer.106.5.1.

Cerf, M., Greenleaf, E., Meyvis, T., & Morwitz, V. G. (2015). Using Single-Neuron Recording in Marketing: Opportunities, Challenges, and an Application to Fear Enhancement in Communications. *Journal Of Marketing Research (JMR)*, *52*(4), 530–545. doi:10.1509/jmr.13.0606.

Creusen, M. E., & Schoormans, J. P. (2005). The different roles of product appearance in consumer choice. *Journal of Product Innovation Management*, *22*(1), 63–81.

Dickins, T. E. (2005). Challenging the rational choice theorist perspective. In Dylan Evans and Pierre Cruse (Eds.) *Emotion, evolution and rationality*. Oxford: Oxford University Press, No. of pages 292. ISBN 0-19-852898-1. (paperback). *Applied Cognitive Psychology*, *19*(3), 375–377. doi:10.1002/acp. 1096.

Edelman, R. (2011, 15 April). PR, not communications. *6AM blog*. Retrieved from www.edelman.com/p/6-a-m/pr-not-communications/.

Falkow, S. (2016, 6 January). Digital PR content – campaign or conversation? *The Proactive Report*. Retrieved from http://proactivereport.com/digital-pr-content-campaign-or-conversation/.

Forteza, P. (2017, 18 June). @PaulaForteza. *Twitter*. Retrieved from https://twitter.com/PaulaForteza.

Frankl, V. E. (1986). *The doctor and the soul: From psychotherapy to logotherapy*. eBook. New York: Vintage Books.

Friedman, M., & Friedman, R. D. (1990). *Free to choose: A personal statement*. San Diego: Harcourt Brace Jovanovich.

Glasser, W. (1998). *Choice theory: A new psychology of personal freedom.* New York: HarperCollins Publishers.

Glimcher, P. W., Kable, J., & Louie, K. (2007). Neuroeconomic studies of impulsivity: now or just as soon as possible? *The American Economic Review, 97*(2), 142–147.

Grammer, K., Fink, B., Müller, A. P., & Thornhill, R. (2003). Darwinian aesthetics: Sexual selection and the biology of beauty. *Biological Reviews Of The Cambridge Philosophical Society, 78*(3), 385–407.

Gross, J. J. (1998). The emerging field of emotion regulation: An integrative review. *Review of General Psychology, 2*(3), 271–299. Retrieved from www.elaborer.org/psy1045d/cours/Gross(1998).pdf.

Grunig, J. E. (2006). Furnishing the edifice: Ongoing research on public relations as a strategic management function. *Journal of Public Relations Research, 18*(2), 151–176.

Hajszan, T., Dow, A., Warner-Schmidt, J. L., Szigeti-Buck, K., Sallam, N. L., Parducz, A., & Duman, R. S. (2009). Remodeling of hippocampal spine synapses in the rat learned helplessness model of depression. *Biological Psychiatry, 65*(5), 392–400. Retrieved from www.ncbi.nlm.nih.gov/pmc/articles/PMC2663388/.

Hodgson, G. M. (2010). Choice, habit and evolution. *Journal of Evolutionary Economics, 20*(1), 1–18.

Holtman, R. B. (1950). *Napoleonic propaganda.* Baton Rouge, LA: Louisiana State University Press.

Hove, T., & Paek, H. J. (2017). The personal dimensions of public relations' ethical dilemmas. *Journal of Media Ethics, 32*(2), 86–98. Retrieved from www.researchgate.net/profile/Thomas_Hove/publication/315499142_The_Personal_Dimensions_of_Public_Relations_Ethical_Dilemmas/links/58d30b5fa6fdccd24d43c039/The-Personal-Dimensions-of-Public-Relations-Ethical-Dilemmas.pdf.

Howell, G. V., & Miller, R. (2010). Maple Leaf Foods: Crisis and containment case study. *Public Communication Review, 1*(1), 47–56.

Jones, A. G., & Ratterman, N. L. (2009). Mate choice and sexual selection: What have we learned since Darwin? *Proceedings of the National Academy of Sciences, 106*(Supplement 1), 10001–10008.

Kable, J. W., & Glimcher, P. W. (2007). The neural correlates of subjective value during intertemporal choice. *Nature Neuroscience, 10*(12), 1625–1633.

Kalenscher, T. (2007). Choosing is feeling – the cognitive neuroscience of decision making. *Lancet Neurology, 6*(1), 26–27. doi:10.1016/S1474-4422(06)70673-1.

Kierkegaard, S., Hannay, A., & Eremita, V. (2004). *Either/or.* eBook. London: Penguin Books.

Lenin, V. I., & Christman, H. M. (1987). *Essential works of Lenin: 'What is to be done?' and other writings.* New York: Dover Publications.

Lerner, J. S., & Keltner, D. (2000). Beyond valence: Toward a model of emotion-specific influences on judgement and choice. *Cognition & Emotion, 14*(4), 473–493.

Levy, D. J., & Glimcher, P. W. (2012). The root of all value: A neural common currency for choice. *Current Opinion in Neurobiology, 22*(6), 1027–1038.

Louie, K., LoFaro, T., Webb, R., & Glimcher, P. W. (2014). Dynamic divisive normalization predicts time-varying value coding in decision-related circuits. *Journal of Neuroscience, 34*(48), 16046–16057.

Lu, V. (2013, 5 April). Nudge here, nudge there, can bring behaviour change. *Toronto Star.* Retrieved from www.thestar.com/business/2013/04/05/nudge_here_nudge_there_can_bring_behaviour_change.html.

Ly, K., Mazar, N., Zhao, M., & Soman, D. (2013, 15 March). A practitioner's guide to nudging. Report. Rotman School of Management, University of Toronto. Retrieved from www.rotman.utoronto.ca/-/media/…/GuidetoNudging-Rotman-Mar2013.pdf.

Markovitch, N., Netzer, L., & Tamir, M. (2017). What you like is what you try to get: Attitudes toward emotions and situation selection. *Emotion, 17*(4), 728–739.

Marlatt, L. (2014). The neuropsychology behind choice theory: Five basic needs. *International Journal of Choice Theory and Reality Therapy, 34*(1), 16–21.

Marx, K. (1994). On the Jewish question. In K. Marx & L. H. Simon *Selected writings*. eBook. Indianapolis, IN: Hackett.

Maule, S. (2015, 10 September). A nudge and a think. *PR Week*. Retrieved from www. prweek.com/article/1363503/nudge-think-applying-behavioural-science-pr.

McLuhan, M., & Gordon, W. T. (2013). *Understanding media: The extensions of man.* eBook. New York: Gingko Press.

Mill, J. S., & Robson, Ann P. and John M. (1977). On Liberty. In *The Collected Works of John Stuart Mill*, Volume XVIII. Kindle Book. Indianapolis, IN: Liberty Fund, Inc. Toronto: University of Toronto.

Pfau, M., & Wan, H. (2006). Persuasion: an intrinsic function in public relations. In C. H. Botan and V. Hazleton (Eds.) Public Relations Theory II. Mahweh, NJ: Lawrence Erlbaum Associates, pp. 101–136.

Rouhollahi, M. (2016). Choice theory: investigating human behavior in four dimensions. *International Journal of Choice Theory and Reality Therapy, 36*(1), 31.

Sakamoto, K., Laine, T., & Farber, I. (2013). Deciding whether to deceive: Determinants of the choice between deceptive and honest communication. *Journal of Economic Behavior & Organization, 93*, 392–399.

Santayana, G. (1990). *Scepticism and animal faith: Introduction to a system of philosophy*. New York: Dover Publications.

Sen, A. (2012). The reach of social choice theory. *Social Choice and Welfare, 39*(2), 259–272.

Shafir, E., Simonson, I., & Tversky, A. (1993). Reason-based choice. *Cognition, 49*(1), 11–36.

Siddiqui, I. A. (2016, 11 December). Tyagi refers to then PMO. *Telegraph India*. Retrieved from www.telegraphindia.com/1161211/jsp/frontpage/story_124152.jsp.

Smith, A. (1759). *The theory of moral sentiments*. Edinburgh: A. Kincaid and J. Bell. eText. Oxford University. Retrieved from http://ota.ox.ac.uk/text/3189.html.

Stott, J. J., & Redish, A. D. (2015). Representations of value in the brain: An embarrassment of riches? *PLOS Biology, 13*(6), e1002174.

Strait, C. E., Sleezer, B. J., & Hayden, B. Y. (2015). Signatures of value comparison in ventral striatum neurons. *PLOS Biology, 13*(6), e1002173.

Takahashi, T. (2005). Loss of self-control in intertemporal choice may be attributable to logarithmic time-perception. *Medical Hypotheses, 65*(4), 691–693. Retrieved from https://133.87.26.249/dspace/bitstream/2115/46766/1/MH65-4_691-693.pdf.

Thaler, R. H., & Sunstein, C. R. (2009). *Nudge: Improving decisions about health, wealth, and happiness*. London: Penguin Books.

Thaler, R. H. (2016). *Misbehaving: The making of behavioral economics*. NY: Norton.

Van der Laan, L. N., De Ridder, D. T., Viergever, M. A., & Smeets, P. A. (2012). Appearance matters: Neural correlates of food choice and packaging aesthetics. *PLOS one, 7*(7), e41738.

Wang, Z., Li, Y., Childress, A. R., & Detre, J. A. (2014). Brain Entropy Mapping using fMRI. *PLOS one, 9*(3), 1–8. doi:10.1371/journal.pone.0089948.

Weilbächer, R. A., & Gluth, S. (2017). The interplay of Hippocampus and Ventromedial Prefrontal Cortex in memory-based decision making. *Brain Sciences (2076–3425)*, *7*(1), 1–15. doi:10.3390/brainsci7010004.

Wood, W., & Neal, D. T. (2007). A new look at habits and the habit-goal interface. *Psychological Review*, *114*(4), 843–863.

Xenophon, & Ambler, W. (2001). *The education of Cyrus*. Ithaca, NY: Cornell University Press.

YouTube. (2017). Maple Leaf Food Safety. Retrieved from www.youtube.com/results?search_query=maple+leaf+food+safety.

7 Expanding individuality

From human to machine

The role of PR

PR expands individuality by influencing the way information and views are collected, interpreted, communicated and remembered. The effort is unremitting and affects the mind's biology, not only the society it encounters.

Expansion occurs because PR is a persuasive agent. It encourages mental plasticity and complex thoughts and actions, expanding our power to act in more varied ways. In general this is thought a good attribute as when Shakespeare praises Cleopatra's 'infinite variety' (Shakespeare, 1988, p. 1011). A more varied self is a result of accepting changes but the old adage that change comes from within is unhelpful in light of new knowledge, and not enough to see PR's impact. Enhancement of mental capability depends on communicated encounters – between the world within the individual and the world outside, for instance. PR's part in this is itself about to be enlarged by science and technology. For that reason PR needs to know more about why individuals can accept and add to their infinite variety; both individual humans, and soon individual machines. Individuality is not eternally reserved for humans.

We have seen individuality affected by PR's presence in power relations and choice-making; by PR's ability to help the mind use emotion and reason, and subjectivity and objectivity, collaboratively and not in opposition; by PR's ability to satisfy the individual's inherent thirst for data and for answers which raise more questions, prompting more communication; by connecting the external world of organizations to the interior space of individuals. Finally, PR applies powerful technology to communication and takes humans beyond their evolutionary, instinctual and biological limits.

These activities expand human faculties, creating complex connections between individuality and society. Operating in more diverse communication environments the individual can create more identities for different circumstances; express diverse views on subjects transient or fundamental, contradictory or consistent. These outcomes inevitably affect the 'invisible, intertwining structure of groupings and associations', which 'is the mechanism by which democracy has organized its group mind and simplified its mass thinking' (Bernays, 2005, p. 44).

Up to now PR's contribution to expansion assumes the individual and mass mind are connected, and that the way to the individual is through the conforming authority of a larger mass. The intertwining structure needs communicated information to cement a group identity. For that reason PR historically augments individuality by linking it to a mass or group 'mind'. It is useful to ask what this approach has broadly achieved up to now, how it might change, and what this means for enlarging individuality.

For the purposes of the subject 'infinite variety' is enlarging the individual's ability to be more various – to embrace individuality in more and more ways, and more and more powerfully. It is an expanded 'diversity of the self', which does sometimes connect with 'diversity of the group'. PR's power to enlarge this aspect of individuality can be seen by understanding its connection to neural factors; to historical change; to technology and to what individual expansion is and could look like in future.

Neural factors

Plasticity

Individual enhancement requires 'neural and cultural plasticity', an organic mind–brain explanation for the individual's response to exterior experience, and the need to publicly express that response (Malafouris, 2009, p. 256). Elsewhere the idea of plasticity has produced 'neuroanthropology', and 'neuroarchaeology' which is a development from the field of cognitive archaeology. All are useful for understanding how managed public communication affects neural and cultural plasticity. Understanding the neural pathway between exterior change and interior augmentation presents PR with new practical possibilities, by learning how the nervous system adapts to newness, including cultural or technological innovation:

> New styles, materials, manufacture techniques, and cultural practices would put novel demands on the bodies and brains of people making and using these objects.
>
> (Malafouris, 2009, p. 257)

It has already been seen that it is not too much to anticipate a field of 'neuro-PR'. Its activities might involve observing neural plasticity and cognitive interpretations of significant challenges or opportunities. The next stage would be using that knowledge to stimulate plasticity and change an individual's prevailing attitudes, and finally encouraging that individual to promote change still more widely.

Equally important to PR is the individual's desire to *resist or limit* enhancement. Resistance must also be communicated and on a scale convincing to wider publics because of the current interdependence of individual and groups. In either situation, the possibility of improved cognition forces collaboration between the group and the individual. The agent between them is communication, managed or otherwise:

Cognition is not just a solipsistic process but deeply social and enculturated, the fact that material culture does not just constitute a neutral scene for cognitive training but equally inhibits change, and the fact that the material dimension does something significantly different than the conceptual.

(Løvschal, 2014, p. 418)

Biased attention and variable cultural values

Individual reactions to PR-inspired enhancement (or resistance to it) might in future be understood by the biochemistry of two factors: biased attention and variable cultural values. 'Biased attention towards negative or positive material' is:

A useful cognitive endophenotype [an internal behaviour with a potentially clear genetic link] that is easy to obtain and correlates strongly with normal variations in personality traits that are linked to emotional resilience and vulnerability.

(Fox, Ridgewell & Ashwin, 2009, p. 1747)

The effects on attention bias of newly communicated material may include altering levels of serotonin, the neurotransmitter well-known for its part in regulating mood including happiness or stress in relevant areas of the brain. Fox et al. found 'allelic variation on the 5-HTTLPR gene' (an allele is one of usually two positive forms of a gene), the gene that codes for the serotonin transporter which interacted with biases under attention. Two 5-HTTLPR alleles varied according to perceptions of positive or negative material (Fox et al., 2009, p. 1749), with the S allele generally considered responsible for 'negative affect and related disorders' (Chiao & Blizinsky, 2009, p. 3).

It is interesting to PR – and hinted at by its historical practice, as we shall shortly see – that the neuroscience of biased attention may inform the neuroscience behind variable cultural values. It is possible that the balance between individualistic and collectivist cultural values affects the action of serotonin (Chiao et al., 2009). High S allele-carrying Asian populations do not appear as prone as western populations to the same levels of individual stress and mood disorders (Chiao et al., 2009). This has been attributed by some to the influence of Asia's more collectively inclined cultures on the individual's psychopathology (mental health and its disorders). Differences in the S allele have also been found within several European populations (Noskova et al., 2008). Other variable findings between the US and South Korea have been reported for *OXTR* rs53576, a gene connected to 'socio-emotional sensitivity', indicating that 'psychological distress and culture are important moderators that shape behavioral outcomes associated with *OXTR* genotypes' (Kim et al., 2010, p. 15717).

If this is the case, to influence brain chemistry a culture (which in the above cases also happen to be national or regional cultures) needs different sorts of PR to link internal and external experience, to uphold an existing group culture or prepare its members to accept more variety and communicate the change across multiple media. Strictly in PR terms connecting biased attention with cultural variability is roughly equivalent to an '*exo*phenotype', an *external* 'symptom' or behaviour ultimately linked to a gene. In this case the external symptoms are behaviours prompted by PR, rather than by an internal 'disorder' which is the usual clinical definition (McArthur & Borsini, 2009, p. xix).

Enhancement of the individual mind (and PR's impact) depends on accepting or resisting change. Connections between change and human biology are often overlooked in PR, but there is reason to suppose that change-related PR produces cognitive exo- and endophenotypes (internal symptoms) by influencing the biochemistry of the individual via determinate constituents of the mind–brain.

By publicizing causes, brands, celebrities, states, reputation and products PR manages the face of 'newness' and public communication to encourage or resist it. Success depends on the 'production of meaning' (Lende & Downey, 2012, p. 4). PR becomes an appeal to our neural faculties, at present by defining newness to group identities using sophisticated 'symbolic thinking' (Malafouris, 2010, p. 51), by exploiting the places where 'human technological, social and linguistic capacities evolved together in a mutually reinforcing way' (Malafouris, 2010, p. 57). The importance of such communication to understanding a neuroscience of enhancement is readily accepted in archaeology:

> Significant cognitive changes are the product of engagement processes between people and the material world realized in different trajectories of cultural development.
>
> (Malafouris, 2009, p. 257)

There are impediments to understanding how PR changes individuality by changing biochemistry in history or prehistory. For example, the brains of ancient humans must be inferred through the meaning communicated by their art and artefacts that we cannot fully understand. 'It is extremely difficult to classify behavior under the qualitative category of "modernity"' (Garofoli & Haidle, 2013, p. 28). Nevertheless attention bias, variable cultural values and communication appear to have worked together across history and prehistory, and biologically affected the brain: 'evidence shows that adaptive evolution has accelerated in humans and that genes related to psychiatric conditions are highly differentiated across human populations' (Eisenberg & Hayes, 2010, p. 329).

PR's contributions to individuality might also be exposed by a 'cultural neuroscience' exploring the communication origins of change and adaptability, and the link between the individual mind and group influence:

> Psychological and neural architecture that facilitates cultural transmission varies depending on whether the communication of social knowledge occurs within or between members of distinct groups.
>
> (Chiao, Cheon, Pompattananangkul, Mrazek & Blizinsky., 2013, p. 12)

Individuality may be neurally enhanced when a challenging change is communicated. The impulse is biological, the means mechanical, the consequences social and biological. It seems highly likely that PR engages with the brain's plasticity, expanding its capacity to accept more variety. Like other kinds of communication, and possibly more directly than them, PR must often communicate challenging social knowledge, and trigger neural and group change. The change can stem from communication over diverse functions, technologies, beliefs or organizations, which influence the individual's overall response. Because PR is uniquely equipped to represent or defy newness, it is responsible for a large and changing amount of augmentation, continuously adding to or subtracting from individuality's 'infinite variety' in public and private life. The continuous communication of change is PR's perennial responsibility. PR is one reason why, for the individual as much as society, life: 'not only never is but never can be stationary', to enlarge on an observation from Schumpeter (Schumpeter, 2009, p. 82). Where has this particular bond between the mind and PR – the bond of biological enhancement – historically led human individuality?

Historical factors

Expanding individuality

PR's historical impact on individual enhancement has not attracted much attention as a general question, but its impact is clear in history as well as neurology. That claim that might look inflated to anyone outside PR, especially as PR has had a low historical profile until quite recently (except among some practitioners and PR scholars) in comparison with the attention paid to law, banking and other organizational functions.

Edward Bernays worried that PR lacked a written history, especially since he understood history's PR value. His 1952 book *Public Relations* presented a strong historical narrative to burnish PR's professional credentials. Bernays was in no doubt that 'the origins of public relations go back to earliest times' (Bernays, 1980, p. 11). Its continued evolution depended on complex civilizations and their need to accept and exploit change. Bernays made this implicit assumption by his explicitly progressive views: initially stressing the historical role of controlling the mass through managed public communication; proposing that individualism came of age in classical Greece alongside secularism; defining the growth of a 'two-way street' (Bernays, 1980, p. 5) of communication between groups, people, leaders and followers that further stimulated the role of managed public communication. This trajectory continued in his account, with a few checks, until an industrial, urban, more democratic age made it necessary to closely manage opinion on a still wider array of subjects. PR evolved from a distinct activity without a name into a distinct profession with a name.

Bernays implicitly equated PR with the expansion of individuality and the importance of managing it, and the rise of PR's 'two-way street' between audiences and organizations that he believed distinguished PR from publicity's 'one way street'. This interpretation said individual enhancement was essential to creating sophisticated communication exchange, complemented by a paradoxical need to manage this burgeoning individuality into groups, to maintain social order.

There is much to support this account of individuality's expansion aided and abetted by PR activities. In many places a clear historical trend is the individual's accumulation of powerful ways to receive and distribute views and information. Song, poetry, literacy, the printing press, consumerism, democracy, the internet and so on have expanded individuality's infinite variety, often at PR's hands. The capacity to accept newness and communicate change has historically stimulated knowledge and creativity among individuals and organizations. Campaigning and commercial organizations acknowledge individual selfhood in their PR and advertising, designed for increasingly segmented target publics. The communication relationship between many states and their citizens frequently give at least an impression that the individual is valued, even if only as a contributor to the collective. Corporations work to create an impression of personal connections, knowing private individuals have the communication tools, which means the power, to affect their product and reputation in the public arena. In return, enhanced individuality augmented by media influences corporate PR, which adjusts to the groups and individuals corporations engage with.

All this is familiar, but not the whole story. Historically, PR has a more mixed connection with infinite variety, sometimes expanding, sometimes contracting it with cooperation from individuals themselves since at certain times and places forms of individuality are treated as a threat. Bernays credited a helpfully evolved individuality to classical Greece and a case can be made from the viewpoint of civic life, politics, philosophy and scientific inquiry, some of the most vital features of the modern world. Nevertheless in earlier chapters, evolutionary, neurological, cognitive and historical evidence shows individuality and individualism were encouraged by managed communication long before classical Greece. Media must always appeal to our biological senses and this could be done with premodern media from beads and flutes to organized rituals. It is not quite a parenthesis to recall Marshall McLuhan's daring suggestion that the first medium to stimulate this selfhood in the public domain was 'the sense of smell, long considered the root of memory and the unifying basis of individuality'. It set the individual in a group and formed an obstacle to external change by distracting 'our habits of detachment and specialist attention' (McLuhan & Gordon, 2013, Chapter 15).

The earliest organizations did not know the underlying neuroscience but they knew about strong individuality, its capacity to diversify and spread, and refer experience back to itself, not to external authorities. For that reason premodern public communication often had to persuade or seduce individuality to fold itself into the group (and sometimes did so with the aid of state-approved scent in religious rituals, including aromatic herbs, or gums and resins like frankincense and myrrh). Communicated commands were not enough to maintain successful societies; the senses were evoked too.

If individuality's communication importance was known before classical Greece, after it there were long interruptions to individuality's progress. Renewed impetus came when the Italian Renaissance reinterpreted classical thinkers like Protagoras (see Chapter 2) and joined them to an urban, civic humanism that placed the individual in a space – in an architecture of humanism – designed to encourage individuality's fullest potential. An embodiment of the humanist Renaissance was the architect, artist, scholar and universal man Leon Battista Alberti (1404–72), who addressed his fellow humans thus:

> To you is given a body more graceful than other animals, to you power of apt and various movements, to you most sharp and delicate senses, to you wit, reason, memory like an immortal god.
>
> (Quoted in Translation in Clark, 1969, p. 89)

Accompanying this was an expansion of trade, guilds and businesses, and trading houses whose proprietors protected and communicated their reputation as a necessity for prosperity and posterity. Men like Francesco di Marco Datini (1335–1410), a successful merchant from Prato in northern Italy whose papers survive, evidently took great pains to manage their public identity, sometimes across a city and sometimes across the Mediterranean. A surge of civic art patronage, alms, gifts, service, public parades backed by business people showed that the business of large-scale public communication was no longer confined to servants of the state of the church. People concerned with making money used publicity. Earthly and heavenly success directly depended on their personal and not only corporate reputation (Origo, 1959). It was in effect a new form of commercial individuality, defined by variable blends of humanism, faith and self-publicity, or publicity of the Self. More people communicated their individuality for secular reasons. In 1980 Stephen Greenblatt proposed the term 'self-fashioning' when he wrote of sixteenth century literary England 'that there were both selves and a sense that they could be fashioned' (Greenblatt, 2012, p. 1). Enhanced individuality is again closely connected to the power of communicating it.

In the nineteenth century the Romantic Movement in art and literature, and the industrial production of goods moved individuality closer to the centre of public communication, assisted by popular Social Darwinism. Self-fashioning could assume a heroic lustre on an industrial scale which took it further beyond poets, artists, generals or heads of state, captains of industry, to bring in middle class inventors, working class labourers, consumer products, industrial machines, national events and nations or whole peoples. Samuel Morse and his telegraph, McCormick and his reaper, Camp Coffee, Navy Rum, Capstan Cigarettes all invested their public identity with a heroic sense of mission connected to invigorating ideas about expansion or destiny. Industrial devices like coffee roasters, or materials such as coal could to some extent do the same when they were glorified in the setting of an Imperial or National Exhibition. Ideas about publicizing a client and its audience as heroic remain in use, if checked somewhat by several of the twentieth century's sombre events and fresh doubts about both devices and destiny.

Constraining individuality

Self-fashioning would be very familiar to any westernized culture or PR practitioner today. Individuality is sometimes identified as a particularly western preoccupation (Oyserman, Coon & Kemmelmeier, 2002, p. 3), not necessarily an outcome of technological or commercial conditions that could happen elsewhere. Not that everyone in the west welcomed individuality. The chapter on choice showed that many western thinkers and activists viewed individuality as something to be diluted, not enhanced. Many, Lewis Hinchman wrote in an influential article on 'The idea of individuality' treat 'the emergence of the modern individual as at least contemporary with, if not the cause of, the decay of a thriving public sphere' (Hinchman, 1990, p. 760). The public sphere is more ethical. Individuality is harder to manage, and its infinite varieties do not necessarily fit the plans of organizations or idealists. Eighteenth century French Revolutionaries made individualism into an accusation: *individualisme*, a dangerous ideology threatening the collective purpose. Like Bernays, Hinchman concentrated on the western intellectual tradition, but as so often elsewhere managed public communication is an invisible presence in his work, glimpsed in such observations as 'taken-for-granted aspects of the self *must first be externalized and negated* in order finally to be reassimilated into an emergent individual identity' (Hinchman, 1990, p. 761) [author's italics].

The work of managing public communication to turn positive perceptions of individualism into negative perceptions of *individualisme* is affected by other histories, other diversities. *Individualisme*'s restrictions are not just imposed: like its opposite it uses collaboration between individual and organization. Western oriented analyses of constraint-based public communication frequently overlook alternative possibilities of collaboration and concentrate on command-based top-down communication involving the state, propaganda and a much-battered individual autonomy. Of course the west has experienced totalitarian state propaganda. Protecting individuality from it is considered fundamental to freedom. There is a modern legacy of fear about state communication's threat to the individual, to the point where 'propaganda' became a wholly pejorative word. Propaganda undermines individuality because it is an aesthetically delivered demand, and flags a power imbalance between organization and individual; what President Eisenhower called 'the acquisition of unwarranted influence' in his warning against the military-industrial complex (Eisenhower, 1961). Propaganda's particular effect on individuality famously interested George Orwell in *Animal Farm* and *1984*, and Carl Jung later in life. To Jung it was an influence that 'may cause us to live in ways unsuited to our individual natures' leading to a 'psychic imbalance' (Jung, 1997, p. 35).

Such qualms are not unanimously shared. Hannah Arendt in her noted book *The Origins of Totalitarianism* (1951) believed fear of propaganda's power was more damaging than the reality:

> It is the common error of our time to imagine that propaganda can achieve all things and that a man can be talked into anything provided the talking is sufficiently loud and cunning.
>
> (Arendt, 2004, p. 106)

Along with overstated fear there is little popular understanding that communication by the state can be dynamic and creative even when it is negative or repressive. The authors of a 2001 research paper persuasively predicted:

> Authoritarian regimes will have to continually adapt their measures of control if they want to counter effectively the challenges of future variations in information and communication technologies.
>
> (Kalathil & Boas, 2001, Conclusion)

The effort many totalitarian or single party states like Russia or China now make to adjust their messages to Information Age media, suggest they too value creativity in managed or controlled public communication. The historical effect of creative state-managed propaganda on a willing individuality is not to be overlooked by students of history, politics, psychology, human rights or communication.

While many states have and do look to closely manage individuality, two other caveats must be added to analyses of non-western propaganda and communication management generally. One is the fairly well-known fact that individuality may be viewed differently within some cultures. The other is that propaganda does not exist in a vacuum. Competitive forms of commercial and civic PR are still active in strong Statist cultures. If one form of managed public communication attempts to limit individuality, others are doing the opposite, and the individual's connection with propaganda is muddied.

In China the individual is exposed to a considerable amount of state propaganda, but also to other ideas about individuality, through which PR raises other possibilities for enhancement. Commercial PR appeared in China in the 1980s with the first steps towards economic liberalization and spread slowly out from the special economic zones. A key moment in PR's lift-off in China (as opposed to monopoly state propaganda and information services) is credited to the increased liberalization of commercial print media in 1993, and fading western memories of the Tiananmen Square massacre in 1989, that fateful year for many Communist governments around the world (*The Economist*, 2002). Does that mean, as *The Economist* proposed, that China became: 'A nation of 1.3 billion waiting to be spun' (*The Economist*, 2002)? The answer would seem to be yes, given the development of PR courses in Chinese University, the number of western companies seeking Chinese business and Chinese companies seeking global business, the arrival of PR multinationals in China and now the rise of Chinese companies like the BlueFocus Group, one of the world's biggest PR businesses which by 2017 employed 5,000 people in 100 offices in ten countries (BlueFocus Group, 2017).

The challenge of western-style PR is counterbalanced by state authorities and by the transition of former state officials to commercial PR, and by public readiness to align community and state. In China 'Xuanchuan' ('propaganda' or 'publicity') is not pejorative, and 'is in fact a neutral term free from any derogatory connotations' (Bin, 1998, p. 43). More than in the west, public opinion sets limits to individuality, and is cautious about *individualisme*. A recent study explored climate change perceptions among 515 Beijing residents along a grid of 'individualism–communitarianism (group) and hierarchism–egalitarianism' (Xue, Hine, Marks, Phillips & Zhao, 2016, p. 137). The conclusion: 'higher scores on individualism were associated with reduced support for policies to mitigate climate change' (Xue et al., 2016, p. 142).

In some cultures, popular readiness to markedly restrict individuality by communication is not reinforced by atheist revolutionary ideology but by popular conservative views of religion that come closer to 'religion's' possible Latin derivation – *ligere*: to bind, or connect. Islamic-centred PR shares some of the social motivations of Confucianism, with the difference that a community and its values are validated by a communicated universal faith, rather than by intricate ritual and ancestor veneration. At the same time, several different and contradictory forms of managed public communication encounter each other in many Islamic societies as they do in China, with consequences for individuality's expansion. The Middle East's professional PR sector has for some time included many of the world's biggest agencies (PR Week Staff, 2016) along with a local professional association. Burson-Marsteller's 2017 Arab Youth Survey found respondents more likely to use English in their daily lives and active on social media (ASDA'A Burson-Marsteller, 2017). Openness and a wish to test boundaries might be expected among this group, which makes up 30 per cent of the Arab world (UNDP, 2016, p. 22). A 2016 report for the UN Development Programme recorded an 'explosive rise' of 'self-expressive or individualistic agency' among Arab youth because of media penetration and 'access to knowledge and information, which widens people's intellectual resources, leading them to become cognitively more autonomous', although not at the 'level common in the rest of the world' (UNDP, 2016, p. 49). One reason for this lower level of autonomy is the group's much higher level of piety compared with global counterparts (UNDP, 2016, p. 50). Individual enhancement (or *individualisme*) is checked by a desire to bring the Islamic world into its Ummah, or community, also with help from PR and the media. The 2011 Jakarta Declaration on Media in the Islamic World in 2011 was produced by the Saudi-funded Muslim World League's second international conference on Islamic media, sponsored by the Indonesian Government. It proclaimed Islam's responsibility to 'promote moderation, objectivity, peace, impartiality' and 'to support and defend the causes of the Muslim Ummah, and unite the Muslims' voice and stance'. 'New communication technology' it warned 'could lead to individualism with all the accompanying negative implications' (Muslim World League, 2011). *Principles of Islamic Marketing*, published by Routledge, declares that: 'PR is the task and responsibility of every Muslim within the *Umma* [*sic*]

(Muslim Nation)' and should be based on 'good conduct, mercy and forgiveness, modesty, justice, loyalty and ethics' (Kirat, 2016, p. 100).

There is no doubt about PR's historic role in enhancing individuality, or that its techniques may be used to restrain the process. The latter becomes more likely when essential virtues are credited to an organization or a collectivity of people, rather than – as Jung believed – to the individual's inner life. Will these connected possibilities and the neural processes driving them have any connection to PR in the future, and the expansion of individuality?

Future factors: machine to individual PR

PR has enhanced individuality by its enormous role in interpreting change. Change enlarges the possibilities for communication, which must strengthen or weaken connections between individuals and often-competing groups; communication must often interpret complex information to encourage or force individual reflection and engagement in the public sphere. In such ways PR and its historical antecedents elevated the individual's capacity to express and process information, which contributed to the growth of complex societies. The next expansion, the next possibility for change is to move responsibility for PR to machines capable of engaging individuality, and the next expansion – as far as we can see – is to build individuality into technology, including media technology once made to importune us with managed messages, but which may reverse that relationship by developing new forms of individuality with needs of their own and with huge consequences for PR.

This may happen because media is not the whole of PR's involvement with technology. Popular conviction about technology's potential to transform itself and humans adds to its PR value. Technology plays a part in PR because of its impact on human self-regard. PR has often made technology and science into attractive visions that penetrate individual consciousness. A case could for instance be made that the dazzling Apollo moon project was pursued for PR reasons. US President Kennedy launched the programme in May 1961 as a 'special message to Congress on urgent national needs' a month after the Soviet Union's publicity success in putting the first man into space, which had an immense impact on global opinion and 'the battle that is now going on around the world between freedom and tyranny' (Kennedy, 1961).

What influence does PR have on the future of machines and individuality? Some of the technology being developed was recounted in earlier chapters, but that is merely technology human PR practitioners can apply to reach human individuals. Beyond that is the prospect of machines applying PR themselves with minimal human intervention; the prospect of emotionally intelligent machines engaging one another in persuasion and dialogue with the goal of shaping their perceptions, opinions and actions.

AI and machine learning are of course already at work in PR but still need humans. Perceptions of products, issues or people are influenced by SEO algorithms, retweeting bots, reports and articles written by AI, or automated data mining. It might be supposed such tools will get better and better at penetrating the biochemical elements of individuality, perhaps creating a 'hyper-individuality' unleashed by a more personal attraction to more personal and powerful machines. According to one PR practitioner posting in *Fortune* magazine:

> The more granular our goals become – paired with smaller, more niche audiences, rapidly expanding industries and higher communication expecta-tions – the bigger the need becomes to solve those effectively and effi-ciently. AI cannot do this for us outright, but it will serve as an essential component for the work we do.
>
> (Whitaker, 2017)

Tech-prompted granularity may enrich the 'engineering' component of PR originally described by Bernays in 1947. In this scenario PR's 'engineering of consent' becomes far more granular, embracing 'message engineering' and a more intense application of science to influence people and measure the results. In the words of a report to the UK's Institute of Public Relations (IPR), PR changes 'from a business of relationships to a business of terabytes' (Weiner & Kochhar, 2017, p. 17).

The unspoken assumption behind these views is that individuality continues to matter. A repeated theme in this book is that without the autonomy of individ-uality there is no need to persuade or converse. Without it PR or any kind of per-suasive communication by a group or organization is redundant. In the IPR report, big data ushers in 'a new form of public relations':

> Where statistics spark creativity; data drive more fully integrated communi-cations decision-making; and tools enable people to act more quickly and with greater intelligence.
>
> (Weiner et al., 2017, p. 5)

Technology in other words continues to adjust PR to individuality's expansion, continues to assume that individuality is the preserve of human beings and that human individuality continues to matter to organizations. These last two points are by no means certain. The new technological world opening to PR will obey familiar rules, experienced by older media. It will develop a power of its own which shapes the intended message, as media has always done in the past. It will once again permit individuality to extend itself further into the external world.

Other consequences will be less familiar. A new technology may be able to extend a personality of its own and not express it in communication with the humans it theoretically serves, but in communication with other machines with personalities of their own. This raises the possibility of non-human publics, new kinds of individuality, and new kinds of PR. Machine individuality and its rami-fications for PR are the subjects of the next chapter. After that, the last chapter suggests some consequences of this rapidly approaching step in redefining and enhancing individuality, a step which already seems enormous to society is certainly momentous for PR.

References

Arendt, H. (2004). *The origins of totalitarianism.* New York: Schocken Books.

ASDA'A Burson-Marsteller. (2017). Arab youth survey 2017. Retrieved from http://arabyouthsurvey.com/findings.html.

Bernays, E. L. (1980). *Public relations.* eBook. Norman, OK: University of Oklahoma Press.

Bernays, E. L. (2005). *Propaganda.* New York: Ig.

Bin, Z. (1998). Popular family television and party ideology: The Spring Festival Eve happy gathering. *Media, Culture & Society, 20*(1), 43–58.

BlueFocus Group (2017). Who we are. Company website. Retrieved from www.bluefocusgroup.com/en/gylb/#a1.

Chiao, J. Y., & Blizinsky, K. D. (2009). Culture–gene coevolution of individualism–collectivism and the serotonin transporter gene. *Proceedings of the Royal Society of London B: Biological Sciences,* rspb20091650.

Chiao, J. Y., Cheon, B. K., Pornpattananangkul, N., Mrazek, A. J., & Blizinsky, K. D. (2013). Cultural neuroscience: Progress and promise. *Psychological Inquiry, 24*(1), 1–19. doi:10.1080/1047840X.2013.752715.

Clark, K. (1969). *Civilisation.* New York: Harper & Row.

Economist, The. (2002). Public relations in China: Puffing away. *The Economist,* 29 August. Retrieved from www.economist.com/node/1302555.

Eisenberg, D. T., & Hayes, M. G. (2010). Testing the null hypothesis: Comments on 'Culture-gene coevolution of individualism–collectivism and the serotonin transporter gene'. *Proceedings of the Royal Society of London B: Biological Sciences, 278*(1704), 329–332. Retrieved from http://rspb.royalsocietypublishing.org/content/royprsb/278/1704/329.full.pdf.

Eisenhower, D. D. (1961, 17 January). Farewell address. Retrieved from http://avalon.law.yale.edu/20th_century/eisenhower001.asp.

Fox, E., Ridgewell, A., & Ashwin, C. (2009). Looking on the bright side: Biased attention and the human serotonin transporter gene. *Proceedings of the Royal Society of London B: Biological Sciences, 276*(1663), 1747–1751.

Garofoli, D., & Haidle, M. N. (2013). Epistemological problems in cognitive archaeology: An anti-relativistic proposal towards methodological uniformity. *Journal of Anthropological Sciences = Rivista di Antropologia: JASS/Istituto Italiano di Antropologia, 92,* 7–41. Retrieved from www.isita-org.com/jass/contents/2013vol. 91/garofoli/23648691.pdf.

Greenblatt, S. (2012). *Renaissance self-fashioning: From More to Shakespeare.* Chicago: University of Chicago Press.

Hinchman, L. (1990). The idea of individuality: Origins, meaning, and political significance. *The Journal of Politics, 52*(3), 759–781. Retrieved from www.jstor.org/stable/2131826.

Jung, C. G. (1997). *Man and his symbols.* New York: Doubleday.

Kalathil, S., & Boas, T. C. (2001). The internet and state control in authoritarian regimes: China, Cuba and the counterrevolution. *First Monday, 6*(8).

Kennedy, J. F. (1961, 25 May). Special message to Congress on urgent national needs. Address to Congress. Retrieved from www.jfklibrary.org/Asset-Viewer/Archives/JFK-POF-034-030.aspx.

Kim, H. S., Sherman, D. K., Sasaki, J. Y., Xu, J., Chu, T. Q., Ryu, C., Suh, E. M., Graham, K., Taylor, S. E. (2010). Culture, distress, and oxytocin receptor polymorphism (OXTR) interact to influence emotional support seeking. *Proceedings of the National Academy of Sciences*, *107*(36), 15717–15721. Retrieved from www.pnas.org/content/107/36/15717.full.pdf.

Kirat, M. (2016). An expert's perspective: Public relations in Islam. In Alserhan, B. A. (2016). *The principles of Islamic marketing*. London: Routledge.

Lende, D. H., & Downey, G. (2012). Neuroanthropology and its applications: An introduction. *Annals of Anthropological Practice*, *36*(1), 1–25. Retrieved from www.researchgate.net/profile/Greg_Downey/publication/264291042_Neuroanthropology_and_its_applications_An_introduction/links/54359b0b0cf2643ab9867c59.pdf.

Løvschal, M. (2014). From neural synapses to culture-historical boundaries: An archaeological comment on the plastic mind. *Journal Of Cognition & Culture*, *14*(5), 415–434. doi:10.1163/15685373-12342135.

Malafouris, L. (2009). 'Neuroarchaeology': Exploring the links between neural and cultural plasticity. *Progress in Brain Research*, *178*, 253–261. doi: 10.1016/S0079-6123(09)17818-4.

Malafouris, L. (2010). Metaplasticity and the human becoming: Principles of neuroarchaeology. *Journal of Anthropological Sciences*, *88*(4), 49–72.

McArthur, R. A., & Borsini, F. (2009). *Animal and translational models for CNS drug discovery: Reward deficit disorders*. Burlington, MA: Academic Press.

McLuhan, M., & Gordon, W. T. (2013). *Understanding media: The extensions of man*. New York: Gingko Press.

Muslim World League. (2011, 15 December). The Jakarta Declaration on media in the Muslim world. *The Second International Conference on Islamic Media*. Jakarta, Indonesia. Retrieved from http://en.themwl.org/content/jakarta-declaration-media-muslim-world.

Noskova, T., Pivac, N., Nedic, G., Kazantseva, A., Gaysina, D., Faskhutdinova, G., ... & Kovacic, Z. (2008). Ethnic differences in the serotonin transporter polymorphism (5-HTTLPR) in several European populations. *Progress in Neuro-Psychopharmacology and Biological Psychiatry*, *32*(7), 1735–1739.

Origo, I. (1959). *The merchant of Prato: Francesco di Marco Datini*. London: Reprint Society.

Oyserman, D., Coon, H. M., & Kemmelmeier, M. (2002). Rethinking individualism and collectivism: evaluation of theoretical assumptions and meta-analyses. *Psychological Bulletin*, *128*(1), 3–72.

PR Week Staff, (2016, 2 May). Global agency business report, 2016. *PR Week*. Retrieved from www.prweek.com/article/1391811/rankings-tables-prweek-global-agency-business-report-2016.

Schumpeter, J. A. (2009). *Capitalism, socialism and democracy*. New York: Harperperennial.

Shakespeare, W. (1988). Antony and Cleopatra. In Shakespeare, W., *The complete works: Compact edition*. Oxford: Oxford University Press. 1001–1036.

UNDP. (2016). Arab human development report. NY: United Nations Development Programme. Retrieved from www.arab-hdr.org/reports/2016/english/AHDR2016En.pdf?download.

Weiner, M., & Kochhar, S. (2017). Irreversible: The public relations big data revolution. London: Institute for Public Relations. Retrieved from www.instituteforpr.org/wp-content/uploads/IPR_PR-Big-Data-Revolution_3-29.pdf.

Whitaker, A. (2017, 20 March, 9.00 a.m.). How advancements in artificial intelligence will impact public relations. *Forbes*. Community voice. Retrieved from www.forbes.com/sites/theyec/2017/03/20/how-advancements-in-artificial-intelligence-will-impact-public-relations/#2903641de536.

Xue, W., Hine, D. W., Marks, A. G., Phillips, W. J., & Zhao, S. (2016). Cultural world-views and climate change: A view from China. *Asian Journal Of Social Psychology*, *19*(2), 134–144. doi:10.1111/ajsp. 12116.

8 Machine individuality and machine to machine PR

If individuality matters to organizations in future, what part will PR play in that relationship? The mutual expansion of complex individuality and complex media technology will create more complex and far-reaching communication tasks for organizations. PR is likely to follow individuality as far as it can, which means artificial agents (AAs), machine learning, AI, and technical, technological and scientific approaches. There is little chance in PR that humans will remain 'the measure of all things', to repeat Protagoras. That change is approaching very fast and it is time for PR to think about it in detail, despite the imperfect and constantly-changing available knowledge.

The first step is to accept that change is not fictional or far off. Artificial consciousness seems to be coming. Machines will not just be making things for us, they will be thinking and feeling for and between themselves. They will begin a new relationship with communication, including public communication.

PR has been adjusting itself to science and technology for many years, not always with enthusiasm. One exception was Bernays. He, as briefly mentioned in Chapter 7, called PR practitioners 'consent engineers'. It was a phrase made to capture the prevailing technocratic, planned and scientific post-war approach to managing society, and first appeared in a 1947 essay, which was later expanded into a book, *The Engineering of Consent* (1955):

> Just as the civil engineer must analyze every element of the situation before he builds a bridge, so the engineer of consent, in order to achieve a worthwhile social objective, must operate from a foundation of soundly planned action.
>
> (Bernays, 1947, p. 116)

PR is often faster at adopting 'back office' technology for monitoring, audience analysis and other kinds of research. Its adoption of 'front office' emerging media for engineering consent often trails public preferences. New media technology can be monitored for popularity but early adoption is not always useful. There is little point speaking into a void. Someone must be out there, listening.

Or something. PR must face the possibility that a machine will be the organization or the audience, or the PR practitioner, or all three, plus the media and message: an AA equipped with AI, machine learning abilities and above all with a distinct individuality. It may or may not look humanoid or incorporate human biology. It might, at least to start with, directly or indirectly serve a human need instead of its own, and communicate about it to humans and other machines with which (or with whom?) it must collaborate. PR is already communicating to if not really with this new audience at a basic level, adjusting messages to meet the needs of SEO and twitterbots. Algorithms are created to generate information or disinformation, depending on the needs of the programmer. Achieving cooperation from autonomous devices with publicity power is truly becoming an engineering task, and will in time require yet more 'back office' support from neurology and cognitive sciences. Soon the relevance of those subjects to AI in PR will matter as much as they do to human individuality.

Caution is required:

> No existing approach to artificial consciousness has presented a compelling demonstration of phenomenal machine consciousness, or even clear evidence that artificial phenomenal consciousness will eventually be possible.
>
> (Reggia, 2013, p. 112)

Phenomenal machine consciousness arises within the machine itself, much like epiphenomenal ideas about human consciousness (see Chapter 5). That would be a large and definitive step, but a machine need not replicate human consciousness so exactly in order to be conscious.

> For example, it might be possible to create a system based on biological neurons that was capable of phenomenal states, but lacked the architecture of human consciousness and any of its associated cognitive states or behaviours.
>
> (Gamez, 2008, p. 890)

Nor is the more cautious paper quoted above necessarily sceptical about the whole project:

> We are at the same point today with artificial consciousness as Alan Turing was in 1950 regarding AI: there are many objections to the possibility of instantiated [demonstrable] machine consciousness, but none are as yet compelling.
>
> (Reggia, 2013, p. 128)

'Few would argue with great confidence that the probability [of advanced AI] is negligible' agreed a 2015 document co-written on behalf of leaders in the AI community (Russell, Dewey & Tegmark, 2015, p. 109). This chapter asks how a new individuality, that of machines, might become a factor in PR, and what it means for the individuality of humans.

Machine consciousness and PR

The challenge to PR's understanding of its function

'Of course, human beings themselves lie at the final goal of robotics', the Japanese robotics engineer Masahiro Mori informed readers in a short and influential piece 'The uncanny valley' (Mori, 1970, p. 33). Individual human beings are conscious of their individuality and the groups they belong to, while an AA is probably not yet independently conscious of either except as mechanical functions. If a machine becomes fully conscious of itself, it will be open to persuasion and dialogue and if it is to matter to PR as an audience it will share several characteristics with human consciousness. To be useful to PR artificial consciousness must have the power to make choices or assent to something after reflection, which as F. H. George points out creates an indeterminate state of change in humans that is 'unconnected with the physical determinacy of his brain workings' (George, 1979, p. 43). This kind of indeterminate consciousness may depend on a brain-like function in AA equivalent to an organic brain in humans.

An array of qualities are needed to make conscious, choosing, assenting machine-brains a PR target for dialogue or persuasion instead of commands. A PR-ready machine perhaps has a need for connection with organizations; possesses the vital counterweight of individual autonomy that prevents an organization from effortlessly harnessing it for a purpose; is endowed with curiosity; with a fundamental but unrealizable desire for truth. It has a foundation of beliefs, perhaps a sense of ethics; a sense of fair or unfair treatment; strikes a cooperative balance between emotion and reason; accepts power hierarchies. It can internally assess external information; turn an objective percept into a subjective perception using imagination and opinions of its own; communicate and show sensitivity to symbols and any archetypes they represent.

None of these things necessarily denote consciousness: non-conscious robots can be (are being) machined to imitate but not feel emotion; can absorb information without being independently curious; can take their place in a hierarchy automatically, without self-reflection. Taken together though, and placed in an AA, these characteristics may eventually represent a new addition to the world's community of conscious things, a new form of individuality and new tasks for human or automated PR. Such a machine will not need to look human, or operate in biological collaboration with human beings in the form of conscious prosthetics.

For many people – PR practitioners included – the notion that machines conscious of their selfhood might need or conduct PR seems distant, irrelevant, outlandish. Perhaps that reaction owes something to the 'uncanny valley' idea Masahiro Mori applied to robot design. Our ascent to accepting anything, including robots, he proposed, is obstructed by perceptual gulleys or valleys. These open when the 'safe familiarity' of a thing is suddenly and unsettlingly shaken by 'negative familiarity'. In robots the causes for this include an unnerving 'unhumanlike design' (Mori, 1970, p. 33), that compromises a robot replication. A faux skin texture, or an inconsistent movement may make the humanlike robot seem grotesque, distorted by disorienting details. Like Frankenstein's monster, our repulsion is magnified by the erstwhile resemblance. 'Why do we humans have such a feeling of strangeness?' Mori asked. 'Is this necessary? I have not yet considered it deeply, but it may be important to our self-preservation' (Mori, 1970, p. 34). The uncanny valley has influenced an enormous amount of research. It is as discomfiting to PR as to many other human activities, since the valley is made by a powerful challenge to perception and emotion. According to a 2017 paper:

> The revealed effect suggests that people prefer human-like replicas to be limited to a certain set of characteristics and might not appreciate them to behave in an empathic or social manner. It could be that they worry about losing their supremacy as humans – as suggested by the threat to human distinctiveness hypothesis – or even fear imminent harm from the sophisticated non-human creation.
>
> (Stein & Ohler, 2017, p. 48)

Experiments in 2012 had suggested the effect might be influenced by the divergence between agency and experience: 'Agency is the capacity to do, to plan and exert self-control; experience is the capacity to feel and to sense' (Gray & Wegner, 2012, p. 126). A person, or in this case a humanlike entity, without experience 'makes people uneasy in a way that someone without agency does not' (Gray et al., 2012, p. 127). This definition must be of interest to PR, which works so intimately with feelings and senses. Could PR between AAs alarm and isolate human onlookers by opening an uncanny valley, one that deranges familiar balances between agency and experience?

Mori's proposal for robot designers, at least to start with, was to say: 'We predict that it is possible to produce a safe familiarity by a nonhumanlike design' (Mori, 1970, p. 34). 'Safe familiarity' could enable PR practitioners to start the next revolution in strategically managed public communication by engaging with AA; until the outlandishness feels safely familiar, and the PR function itself is transferred to AA, and is extended to engage with technically and aesthetically advanced humanlike and conscious robots.

Treating machines as individuals

Meanwhile, to be acceptable to PR the choices a conscious machine makes may be influenced by all or some of those characteristics of human consciousness useful to PR that were just described. A communication process inevitably unfolds from that, which helps the AA develop in more complex ways, and evolve an identity of its own different from other machines, just as PR has done for humans. Differentiation raises the need for diverse and perhaps creative approaches to communicating. Conscious machines could probably not be

' "discrete state machines" ', 'which move by sudden jumps or clicks from one quite definite state to another', and lack meaningful intermediate positions (Turing, 1950, p. 439). To have a humanlike consciousness is to exist in a continuum containing the characteristics just mentioned. To have a consciousness appears to produce a variable personality, one equipped to feel sad or happy – more usefully described by one scholar of AI as 'to experience states of conscious satisfaction or suffering (CSS)' (Torrance, 2014, p. 9).

A. J. Turing was not thinking of PR's connection to AI or CSS when he published his famous paper *Computing Machinery and Intelligence* (1950). Still, he raised interesting possibilities for it when he discussed initial forms of mechanical differentiation: 'Instead of trying to produce a programme to simulate the adult mind, why not rather try to produce one which simulates the child's?' (Turing, 1950, p. 456). He asked: 'do we ever come to the 'real' mind, or do we eventually come to the skin which has nothing in it? In the latter case the whole mind is mechanical' (Turing, 1950, p. 455).

The question is important to PR, and has been explored throughout this book, first for human individuality, and now for individuality in machines. PR owes much of its influence to the human mind's indeterminate or epiphenomenal nature, or both. The debate may never be resolved but there is no such problem when the subject is individual machines and not individual humans. To put it another way, Turing asked whether the problem of designing a real mind is only a practical one for individual machines. Can machines have *a* mind of some sort? If not necessarily *the* exact mind possessed by humans, then one approximating to territory PR often inhabits, a realm well described as 'the chiaroscuro of our desires, emotions, pains and delights in terms of informational operations' and which does not wholly engage in 'that bleaching out of happiness and misery from the fabric of our psychology' (Torrance, 2014, p. 17).

If the individual's purported spiritual or emotional qualities can also be built in to artificial consciousness, so much the better. An approximation of consciousness containing all the characteristics just outlined may suffice as far as PR is concerned. Whether approximately or exactly conscious, could the machine mind be close enough to or superior to the human mind that PR becomes a need? For PR, questions about machines with personalities must include: does the machine desire information and opinion to get at the truth of a thing? Does the machine wish to communicate on matters of importance to it? Does the machine value or at least require persuasion and dialogue as part of this activity, on top of factual data? Would this be a scientific, technical task for PR, or would it still have to imaginatively engage other faculties, including unreason and emotion? There should be time to find out, to professionally evolve. A conscious mind is not going to leap into the world fully perfected. It will continue to change, perhaps creating many kinds of consciousness as the process unfolds (one hesitates to say 'advances'). Would recognizing a rough form of conscious in a machine audience require PR to respect its individual needs when engaging with it? It is a part of a larger question: if humans learn how to manufacture consciousness, to us a decisive proof of sentience, are we morally compelled to extend it to as many machines as we can? If we are, we must allow them to communicate at a more 'human' level.

Scientists or engineers of all stripes would probably be in no doubt. The sheer challenge itself would be justification enough. PR would be in a different position. Machines managing organizations or products, for instance, may need, 'like' or prefer dialogue and persuasion with other machines managing the affairs of individual humans, and persuade aligned groups of such machines that another group's services, or demands, are important to the humans they represent. Perhaps this will at least be a starting point: perennially adjusting individual machine perceptions on behalf of individual humans, as long as humans matter to the process, at which point the machines may enter into a form of PR between themselves: managing our messages, our media, more effectively than any single individual or group of individuals. The exclusion of human individuality from PR, which is to say from the public sphere, might confirm that we may become the only species that voluntarily abolishes itself, by ceding consciousness, autonomy and public communication to new forms. The human individual transferring a form of consciousness to a machine, assents to a new power structure, and the creation of new symbols or archetypes impenetrable to nearly all but not to the machines. Ceding some part of our autonomy to 'artificial' intelligence cedes ownership of dialogue, persuasion and perhaps ownership of our own selves, or chosen portions of our selves which we have biologically extended into conscious AAs – humanity's latest (last?) extension of itself as McLuhan's media and message. This is by no means an AI uprising; more a sort of osmosis between different sources of consciousness. New kinds of PR activity will show that this is happening, and that communication is at the heart of the whole process.

If each element of consciousness can be broken down to a series of functions, it can conceivably be mechanized, and individualized. F. H. George was one of the first to demonstrate this to a non-specialist audience in his *Philosophical Foundations of Cybernetics* (1979). Beliefs, for example, may be '"relatively permanent states" of the central nervous system' but for AI its core functions must be mechanically convertible:

> Beliefs are those stored memories (however stored) whose contents specify for the organism what may be expected to happen (S2) if certain behaviour (R1) is performed under certain stimulating circumstances (S1).
>
> (George, 1979, p. 94)

Stimuli for machine individuality need not be housed in a brain equivalent, a seat of our individual consciousness. This may not be true of the human brain either, if the wider neural ectoderm beyond the brain extending into the nervous system and skin is finally implicated in conscious intelligence (Dubois, 2010). In that circumstance distinctions between 'Artificial' and 'Natural' intelligence become harder still to maintain, and only apply to the structures *supporting* that intelligence, not the overall being that contains them:

What is natural is the neural support of the natural intelligence, given by the natural brain and body of a human being, and what is artificial is the neural support of the artificial intelligence, given by an artificial brain and body of a robot being.

(Dubois, 2010, p. 244)

The things described here reinforce 'the idea that *at least some artificial agents should certainly be given the moral status that humans enjoy* [original italics]' (Torrance, 2014, p. 23). In that case, it is not a minor issue for either individuality or society that these AAs would need PR, and would in fact desire it. An individual machine with moral status roughly akin to individual humans will need PR as much as its human relative. Its objectives will compete with those of other machines; it will seek competitive advantage; it's conscious state and worldly success is affected by the noise of the world, and the humans or machines that organize that noise into managed public communication. Eventual contact between these two forces in fact seems inevitable given that both outside the world of PR, and inside it as briefly noted earlier, 'the domain of the social is expanding rapidly to include human–AA [artificial agent] and AA–AA interactions' (Torrance, 2014, p. 27). PR is about to be changed by AA's made to 'truly "get" human beings' (Newman, 2017) but will be changed even more by AA's interested in 'getting' themselves and their fellow machines.

The face of machine to machine PR

What does artificial consciousness mean for PR in practice and who doubts PR practice will be changed by it? Artificially conscious machines either replicate or reject many familiar elements of human individuality used to connect with PR, which these pages have described. Now is therefore the moment to consider possible characteristics of machine to machine (M2M) PR.

New diversity

One possibility is more diversity in PR between AAs. F. H. George described cybernetics (the precursor to AI and AA) as 'the science of communication in animals, men and machines' (George, 1979, p. 1), adopting a 1948 definition from one of the field's pioneers (Wiener, 1948, p. 14). George was among the first scientists (authors and playwrights had started much earlier) to forecast that human traits contributing to our diversity: free will, consciousness, creativity, informal spontaneity, could be reproduced by AI. Such machines could therefore become recognizably conscious and incorporate elements that characterize diversity of opinion and action, drastically magnified by technology.

In that situation of highly diverse AAs – often described in science fact and fiction and in other utopian and dystopian prognostications – human diversity could no longer count as a chief PR *raison d'être*. In fields closely or loosely connected to the original cybernetics – including robotics, neuroscience, engineering, cognitive science and AI – advancing machine consciousness may make human diversity less valuable to organizations as a source of labour, opinion, consumption, profit or civic engagement. This in turn could make PR between them and humans less necessary, and M2M PR more necessary. The individual might be left alone by organizations to a far greater extent. Is a world where PR overlooks humans a utopia or dystopia?

More relevant for this inquiry, would a relative dearth of human diversity be the death of human-centred PR? In place of human diversity, AA would be far more diverse, and far more important in communication. For example in soft robots (robots made from polymers capable of crawling or acting like human hands): 'diversity-encouraging techniques could finally enable the creation of creatures far more complex and interesting' (Cheney, MacCurdy, Clune & Lipson, 2013, p. 167). Communication resources may be redirected to the machines. The comparative unimportance of human diversity, at least as an asset for competing organizations to bid for, might strip PR of much of its human-centred creative, persuasive and conversational capabilities. The need to urge, coax, inspire or excite a machine aware of its individuality might be more important. The idea that humans must be persuaded and machines instructed could be reversed to some extent.

For now, perhaps a short time, diverse communication in the public sphere remains the product of manifold diversities in the individual mind, a perspective supported by recent cognitive science, among other disciplines, which has to date drawn less attention in PR. What PR might be shared between machines and humans as more is learned about the individual mind and its connections with managed public communication? One at least would be an understanding of PR that rests on a far more diverse series of disciplines than hitherto. A suggestive proposal, for instance, concentrates on scientific diversity and the idea that a 'Philosophy of Information' is 'a unifying philosophy of the cognition disciplines' (Hemmatazad, 2016, p. 200) including AI, information theory and neuroscience, All are firmly inside PR's sphere of interest. A shared philosophy of information adopted and exploited by AAs could not viably ignore PR's influence on perceived information, since individuality often judges information valueless without experiencing it as communication. A common philosophy of information could lay a much bigger, more diverse intellectual foundation for understanding individuality's place in the information process. The outcome may cultivate shared values and shared power over symbols human and machine need to understand and act on. In that sense understanding PR through many and diverse disciplines recognizes the psychologist and cyberneticist F. H. George and his *Philosophical Foundation of Cybernetics* (1979) which explored common elements of human and machined minds, including receptiveness to communicated symbols:

> In fact, as George notes, we may even view thinking itself as 'a process of manipulating symbolic representations of events, and the process of learning and adapting as a result of these manipulations' (1979, p. 3).
>
> (Hemmatazad, 2016, p. 208)

New hierarchies and transparency

M2M PR could use more hierarchical levels of communication based on the possibilities of many different levels of artificial consciousness. Conscious AAs present non-human possibilities for audience targeting based on the qualities of individuality each machine possesses. A future spectrum of AA consciousness would include 'cases of very close bio-commonality at one end, to simplistic current AI-style behaviour at the other end' (Torrance, 2014, p. 25), with the additional factor of human- and non-human-looking machines. Other research proposes four levels of machine consciousness (MC1–4); MC1 being 'Machines with the external behaviour related to consciousness', to the highest of MC4: 'phenomenally conscious machines' (Gamez, 2008, p. 888).

Adjusting persuasion, dialogue or content to levels of machine consciousness, however they are classified, acknowledges new hierarchies whether the PR practitioner is another machine or not. Transparency would not mean the same thing to all AAs, leading some conscious machines to expect more knowledge than others. M2M PR may for logical reasons operate on a need-to-know basis instead. Organizations will be in the position of managing how much they say to conscious AAs stratified by different levels of consciousness, if not wholly in the dystopian fashion of Huxley's *Brave New World*, then at least according to a standard level of classification set by the organization, and whoever or whatever is running it. Human recipients of AAs' perceptions, messages and media, would similarly benefit or suffer from fine-grained information-sharing decisions taken by the stratified machines themselves, and lying beyond the human individual's control.

A hierarchy of AA consciousness also suggests that the most 'conscious' AAs, as classified by the agents themselves or by humans, will concentrate the most power in M2M PR. They may guide the content and transparency of a PR activity conducted between the machines involving selection of media and messages, and managed levels of dialogue, persuasion and instruction based on recognizing the status of another AA's conscious 'individuality'. As in human-centred PR these hierarchical activities might be designed to promote products and organizations, or manage issues or crises, or personalities. If the areas of PR activity may continue to be familiar, the communication content may not be. Human interactions are already often digitally mediated, and some commentators support the idea of 'developing artificial intelligence to persuade' (Kelly, 2011, p. 324). AAs seeking to persuade each other are unlikely to need humans to persuade on their behalf. It is already possible for machines to develop their own impenetrable language when negotiating with other machines, as a Facebook research team learned in 2017, prompting some media hyperbole and alarm. The team's objective is to create chatbots 'that can reason, converse, and negotiate, all key steps in building a personalized digital assistant' (Lewis, Yarats, Dauphin, Parikh & Batra, 2017). When that happens, humans will presumably be able to transfer more individualized tasks into more individualized machines – or will have to if the reasoning, conversing and negotiating machines are just much better at it.

Will the transfer of human communication capacities simply stop there? Locked into McLuhan's principle, humans might continue extending their individuality into some new media where PR can be conducted. But these media might be low in the hierarchy of machine consciousness – MC1s or 2s. Other digital 'assistants' (if that is what they remain), MC4's with an individuality and high PR abilities of their own, may work more effectively without our input. For M2M PR to be comprehensible to humans, individually conscious machines in a new hierarchical paradigm must always communicate in terms humans can understand on things that humans care about. The Facebook experiment showed this might not happen on all subjects, at all times.

Non-human supervision

New hierarchies lead to Juvenal's famous principle *quis custodiet ipsos custodies* or who guards the guardians. It is important to think about supervising PR (or any organizational function) in an era of machine individuality. A revolution in supervision is in prospect because 'the performance of a group of robots is enhanced by communication among the robots' making communication between them 'not a luxury, but a necessity' (Bekey, 2005, p. 419).

Layers of human supervision traditionally thicken with complexity. The increased numbers of supervisors develop more complex tasks in parallel with their growing authority. Complex administration has been known to distract, subordinate and cramp those doing the actual tasks that the organization was made to do, especially when they involve highly individual assets like creative thinking skills.

Conscious AAs will probably not face that perennial problem given their enormous processing capabilities. They are a challenge to the supervisory appetites of humans administering organizations. AAs will need less continuous if any human supervision, by incorporating into what has been called the 'MOTL [man in the loop] paradigm', permitting 'the system to take on characteristics of organisations that would allow it to better conform to the characteristics desired by the supervisor' (Hexmoor, McLaughlan & Tuli, 2009, p. 75). Individual machines may be conducting PR between themselves to service human and machine needs, and doing so without the day-to-day need for human supervision, since the machines themselves will learn the desired supervision characteristics. They will administer them and execute their PR on our behalf, their behalf, and the organization's behalf, for corporations and civil nonprofits, democratic governments, or states seeking closer control over the communication of non-state organizations.

US Army researchers are among those examining 'shared decision-making' – 'mixed initiative' operations involving human and non-human agents – 'to ensure decision-making that is shared, flexible, and still human-centric' (Barnes, Chen & Hill, 2017, p. 1). The paper's authors recommend that:

In the mixed initiative paradigm, it is necessary to develop protocols that dictate when the human, the agent, or both (collaborative) have decision precedence.

(Barnes et al., 2017, p. 1)

It is not hard to relate these issues to the prospect of AA supervising PR. The connection is clearer still when the authors propose that protocols for joint 'human-[artificial] agent' teams must recognize shared trust, emotion, transparency and communication, and other features familiar to PR:

Language processing from simple commands to complex inferencing is maturing rapidly, making human-agent teams that can communicate with each other feasible in the near future. Future research efforts should address the effects of emotions on human-agent team building, ethical constraints of autonomy, and the promise and perils of machine learning.

(Barnes et al., 2017, p. 22)

What now?

If AAs have a version of consciousness they have a version of individuality. If they have a version of individuality they are conscious of their external environment, have objectives in relation *to* it and have a communication relationship *with* it. In at least some cases that must include planned public communication with organizations, people and other machines. The process might be intensely individualized. Appealing to groups, which may be far more transient, might be less effective than large-scale engagement with individuals equipped with enormous communication capacity. So intelligent machines cannot avoid managed public communication, and PR cannot avoid the rise of M2M PR assuming a continuing human interest in AI, in which individuality is an idea connected to consciousness itself, which does not need to be organically housed.

Naturally, science and engineering would play a larger part in PR activities, and perhaps in creativity as well as message delivery and task analysis. Machine to machine PR may not be PR's last random roll of the dice as a profession, but for now it is as far ahead as we can see. It is easier to see the moral quandaries for humans: problems of control; of autonomous decision-making; of acknowledging the rights of non-organic conscious agents; of AAs' acknowledgement of human rights and what that means for transparent communication, applying creative persuasion and dialogue that respects individuality in all its forms. How will these quandaries affect the business of selling a product, believing an argument or strategically managed truth-telling in a crisis? What happens when the communicating organization is effectively a small number of AAs aware of their individuality, and perhaps has at least a rough version of emotional awareness?

The individual's moment of choice, thirst for true information, desire to make power relations, need to share aspects of individuality with an organization or product are age-old reasons for PR. They could all be dramatically and rapidly altered in the next two decades, first by applying neuroscience and cognitive science to the individual's connection to communication, then by applying that knowledge to the engineering of conscious AI with more kinetic (if not potential) learning power than the human mind. It might be hoped that those original reasons for PR's existence continue to matter, though. At the moment there is no evidence that they will not. Their partnership with managed public communication might help individuals and society navigate the new world that is being built, and also (if there is a place for individual consciousness in any form) imagined and created.

References

Barnes, M., Chen, J., & Hill, S. (2017). Humans and autonomy: Implications of shared decision-making for military operations. Paper. US Army Research Laboratory. MD: ARL. 10.13140/RG.2.2.24620.67207.

Bekey, G. A. (2005). *Autonomous robots: From biological inspiration to implementation and control*. Cambridge, MA: MIT Press.

Bernays, E. (1947). The engineering of consent. *The Annals of the American Academy*, *250*(1), 113–120. Retrieved from www.mcnuttphysics.com/uploads/2/3/6/9/23694535/engineering_of_consent-edward_l_bernays.pdf.

Bernays, E. L. (Ed.) (1955). *The Engineering of Consent*. [Essays, by various authors.] Norman, OK: University of Oklahoma Press.

Cheney, N., MacCurdy, R., Clune, J., & Lipson, H. (2013, July). Unshackling evolution: evolving soft robots with multiple materials and a powerful generative encoding. In *Proceedings of the 15th annual conference on Genetic and evolutionary computation* (pp. 167–174). ACM.

De Sousa, A. (2013). Towards An Integrative Theory of Consciousness: Part 2 (An Anthology of Various Other Models). *Mens Sana Monographs*, *11*(1), 151–209. doi:10.4103/0973-1229.109341.

Dubois, D. M. (2010). Natural and artificial intelligence, language, consciousness, emotion, and anticipation. *AIP Conference Proceedings*, *1303*(1), 236–245. doi:10.1063/1.3527159.

Edelson, M., Sharot, T., Dolan, R. J., & Dudai, Y. (2011). Following the crowd: brain substrates of long-term memory conformity. *Science*, *333*(6038), 108–111.

Gamez, D. (2008). Progress in machine consciousness. *Consciousness and Cognition*, *17*(3), 887–910.

George, F. H. (1979). *Philosophical foundations of cybernetics*. Tunbridge Wells: Abacus Press.

Gray, K., & Wegner, D. M. (2012). Feeling robots and human zombies: Mind perception and the uncanny valley. *Cognition*, *125*(1), 125–130. doi:10.1016/j.cognition.2012.06.007.

Hemmatazad, N. (2016). On the diversity of the cognition disciplines and the development of a unifying philosophy of information. *Metaphilosophy*, *47*(2), 199–213.

Hexmoor, H., McLaughlan, B., & Tuli, G. (2009). Natural human role in supervising complex control systems. *Journal of Experimental & Theoretical Artificial Intelligence*, *21*(1), 59–77. doi:10.1080/09528130802386093.

Kelly, A. R. (2011). Book review essay: Persuasion, emotion, and interdisciplinarity. A review of two perspectives. *Communication Review*, *14*(4), 321–325. doi:10.1080/107 14421.2011.624035.

Lewis. M., Yarats, D., Dauphin, Y. N., Parikh, D., & Batra, D. (2017, 14 June). Deal or no deal? Training AI bots to negotiate. Facebook Artificial Intelligence Research. Retrieved from https://code.facebook.com/posts/1686672014972296/deal-or-no-deal-training-ai-bots-to-negotiate/.

Mori, M. (1970). The uncanny valley. *Energy*, *7*(4), 33–35. Retrieved from www.movingimages.info/digitalmedia/wp-content/uploads/2010/06/MorUnc.pdf.

Müller, V. (2012, May). Introduction: Philosophy and Theory of Artificial Intelligence. *Minds & Machines*. pp. 67–69. doi:10.1007/s11023-012-9278-y.

Newman, D. (2017, 24 May). The case for emotionally intelligent AI. *Forbes*. Retrieved from www.forbes.com/sites/danielnewman/2017/05/24/the-case-for-emotionally-intelligent-ai/#1857861c7788.

Paul-Choudhury, S. (2016). Outsmarted? *New Scientist*, *230*(3079), 18–19.

Reggia, J. A. (2013). The rise of machine consciousness: studying consciousness with computational models. *Neural Networks: The Official Journal of the International Neural Network Society*, *44*112–131. doi:10.1016/j.neunet.2013.03.011.

Russell, S., Dewey, D., & Tegmark, M. (2015). Research priorities for robust and beneficial artificial intelligence. *AI Magazine*, 36(4), 105–114. Retrieved from https://futureoflife.org/data/documents/research_priorities.pdf?x57718.

Stein, J., & Ohler, P. (2017). Venturing into the uncanny valley of mind-The influence of mind attribution on the acceptance of human-like characters in a virtual reality setting. *Cognition*, *16*043–50. doi:10.1016/j.cognition.2016.12.010.

Torrance, S. (2014). Artificial consciousness and artificial ethics: Between realism and social relationism. *Philosophy & Technology*, *27*(1), 9–29. doi:10.1007/s13347-013-0136-5.

Turing, A. (1950). Computing machinery and intelligence. *Mind*, *59*(236), 433–460. Retrieved from www.jstor.org/stable/2251299.

Wiener, N. (1948). Cybernetics. *Scientific American*, *179*(5), 14–19. Retrieved from www.jstor.org/stable/24945913.

9   PR and the fate of individuality

PR affects the individual's fate, influence and autonomy because it confirms that individuality matters. PR is the most effective method so far known to communicate *en masse* on diverse subjects while recognizing individuality is autonomous. That is why PR frequently if imperfectly uses advocacy, persuasion and dialogue. Commands do not respect individual influence and autonomy; unadulterated raw data on an enormous scale is hard for audiences to interpret and connect to personal experience. PR tries to build relationships directly or through an identity the individual shares with a group.

For these reasons PR's influence on individuality itself is on the whole positive. Sometimes PR tries to make a passive social 'mass' or 'herd' obedient to a product, person, cause or organization; or less cynically to encourage productive social cooperation; but this is not the sum of what PR does.

Few organizational activities can be more closely bound to individuality than PR. This book has proposed that PR's impact on individuality goes much deeper than the immediate content of its daily operations. Less PR activity may mean that the individual's autonomous status is being reduced. PR and the tales it tells (including the noble lies and ignoble truths) vanish when the most intensely individual features of our common humanity no longer matter to an organization's objectives and its power-holders.

So far, the opposite has happened. This book has examined PR's impact on the long expansion of individuality's public power, including individuality's ability to dilute its autonomy among groups, or to concentrate it back into itself. That ability grows when, as described throughout this book, more powerful media devices pass into individual hands. PR's future relationships with audiences will be much more personal because of this technology, assuming human or other kinds of individuality continue to matter to organizations. For now it is vital for PR to consider its evolving relationship with individuality.

'Public relations': the name of the practice might change in future but at the present time it is perfectly chosen, and possibly essential since individuality itself will not be confined to humans or other purely biological organisms. PR will follow it into the age of conscious AAs. It must. PR denotes something unpredictable, independent and uncertain about individuality that an organization cannot ignore, eradicate, temporarily suppress, cannot take for granted and must relate to if it is to reach many of its goals. In that and others ways about to be described, PR still has tasks to perform.

Escaping exactitude

To be uncertain is to be individual. Uncertainty guides our shifting loyalties and principles; our feckless and measured choice-making. It is a natural counterweight to the communication of certainty by individuals and organizations.

PR is used either to resolve or increase uncertainties among people but success is not guaranteed, especially in more uncertain times. Bernays openly declared in the 1920s, in the boom, bust and political instability between the two world wars, that PR 'can never be an exact science'; 'there must always be a wide margin for error' because it 'deals with human beings' (Bernays, 2005, p. 73). Bernays followed Trotter and Le Bon into the group, not individual, mind. The group mind 'does not *think* in the strict sense of the word. In place of thoughts it has impulses, habits and emotions' (Bernays, 2005, p. 73). While this is discomfiting for business, the idea of uncertainty as an influential space for individuals is more discomfiting. Groups can be managed with greater ease and more economically.

The economic advantages gained from the perpetual management and definitive understanding of individuality eludes PR and organizations. Not even economics itself has come to an unshakeable, exact understanding of people, although it keeps trying. A founder of the Chicago School of Economics, Frank Knight, noted wryly in 1921 that it was 'the only one of the social sciences which has aspired to the distinction of an exact science' and 'secures a moderate degree of exactness only at the cost of much greater unreality' (Knight, 1921, 1.1.1). In 1926 John Maynard Keynes credited 'many of the greatest economic evils of our time' to 'risk, uncertainty, and ignorance' (Keynes, 2013, p. 172). Keynes and Knight are two of the main sources for studying human uncertainty in economics, which modern behavioural economists seek to understand, some presumably to tame it. Earlier still, Marx and Engels' *Communist Manifesto* shared the same purpose, brilliantly capturing the 'everlasting uncertainty and agitation' of the 'bourgeois epoch' (Marx, Engels & Hobsbawn, 1998, p. 38). To Marx uncertainty was a monstrosity; to business it is an inefficiency to be checked and channelled. To PR it is a *raison d'etre*, and a foundation of the individual's ability to make economic and social choices. In return, PR's existence is one of individuality's guarantees of what could be called 'autonomous inexactitude' in the public arena. Today it is possible to agree with one scholar of business uncertainty: 'Uncertainty is increasingly a feature of the real world, considerably more so than it was when economic theory was first formalised in the late 19th century' (Ormerod, 2015, p. 16). PR is the historic acknowledgement of individuality and uncertainty's power in society. And there may be productive benefits for organizations. The economist Armen Alchian said as much in his influential paper 'Uncertainty, evolution and economic theory' (1950), which saw value in 'a type of individual motivated behavior based on the pervasiveness of uncertainty and incomplete information' (Alchian, 1950, p. 211).

Uncertainty interests PR partly for the same reason. In the final analysis understanding the mind may help it manage individuals more closely, but not make them wholly predictable. PR's future expansion could be an organizational response to expanding individual autonomy, but individuality is not exactly something PR celebrates, or accepts as a condition for its own existence.

The continuation of individuality and uncertainty are conditions for PR's future. So is the growing body of knowledge produced by neuroscience, biology and the bridge to action represented by cognitive science, psychology or pharmacology. It is true that caution is needed, another point elaborated on in earlier chapters. PR must heed one scientist's caution that 'pictures of blobs on brains seduce one into thinking that we can now directly observe psychological processes' (Henson, 2005, p. 228) and knows all too well 'the Seductive Allure of Neuroscience Explanations' (Weisberg, Keil, Goodstein, Rawson & Gray, 2008) including the persuasive power of what some scientists have called ' "placebic" information'. 'Any meaningless terminology, not necessarily scientific jargon, can change behavior' (Weisberg et al., 2008, p. 476).

There is still a lot to learn, and this book has tried to show that a lot is being found out, and that new technology is available for PR to test the new knowledge of the mind. A lot to learn, and much of it must be acted on once it is discovered, but for now uncertainty persists and cannot be pinned down. It is thankfully hard for science and PR to map the mind with exactitude and know what it is, or indeed where it is, and what consciousness itself is, which would lead in PR to the appalling competitive necessity of 'persuading' individuals with chemical or technological mind-management. Science is not equipped to explain uncertainty and its biological connections to perception, feeling and human action. The late David Marr (1945–80) at MIT applied AI and neuroscience to explore vision, and warned about the shortcomings with an oft-quoted remark:

> Trying to understand perception by understanding neurons is like trying to understand a bird's flight by studying only feathers. It just cannot be done.
>
> (Marr, 1982, p. 27)

Other neuroscientists share this view. 'The gap between circuits and behavior is too wide to be bridged without an intermediate stage' one commented in 2012 (Carandini, 2012, p. 509). 'Ion channels do not beat, heart cells do' another group reminded readers in 2017. 'Neural circuits do not feel pain, whole organisms do' (Krakauer, Ghazanfar, Gomez-Marin, MacIver & Poeppel, 2017, p. 485). In the hands of PR and new media, incomplete or misunderstood knowledge about the individual mind may be more dangerous and tragic than no knowledge at all. The scientific method may in the end not be equipped to unravel individuality, and less empirical approaches in history, psychology or philosophy may retain their value. The just-quoted paper itself seems to agree.

'There is no escape from philosophy. Every scientist takes a philosophical position, either tacitly or explicitly, whenever they state that a result is "important," "fundamental," or "interesting."' (Krakauer et al., 2017, p. 485):

> The neural basis of behavior cannot be properly characterized without first allowing for independent detailed study of the behavior itself.
>
> (Krakauer et al., 2017, p. 488)

Neuroscience and its related disciplines are not yet equipped to overcome the uncertainty in human action that PR thrives on and at the same time tries to resolve. For now, supercharged by technology, PR does what it can in an intermediate stage somewhere between invasive interventions in neural circuits and surrender to random human behaviours. The acceptance of uncertainty is one way PR preserves individual independence and encourages the further evolution of complex forms of selfhood.

> If man knew the future, he would not have to choose and would not act. He would be like an automaton, reacting to stimuli without any will of his own.
>
> (von Mises, 1949/1966, p. 105)

Accepting hybrid individuality

Although a final, practical, revelation looks unlikely, von Mises' mention of an automaton reminds us much more must be learned if future PR is to work with individuality. One task for PR will be to recognize and legitimize other kinds of individualities. 'If the ways biologists study biological processes are sensitive to what they consider to be individuals,' one philosopher suggests, 'then being correct about which objects are individuals will make for better ways of studying biological processes' (Kovaka, 2015, p. 1096). This recommendation applies to students of PR as well, especially with the prospect of 'biomedia' and artificial consciousness. PR will learn to build new relationships with new individuals. It is now on the brink of entering the individual's biology, and eventually passing beyond it to contact artificial forms of individuality that are technologically and intellectually far more effective and powerful than homo sapiens, and consequently more important to organizations.

McLuhan's theory of media as an extension or prosthetic of the individual, presents PR with a staging post on the route to dealing with complete artificial consciousness. Some of the technology that could accomplish hybridity was briefly described in other chapters, with the caveat that it is going to be outdated by new innovation. This includes the 'memory prosthesis' brain implant introduced at the 2017 Society for Neuroscience meeting in Washington DC which is credited with enhancing human memory for the first time, by mimicking the way it is processed naturally. The device sends small electric shocks into the hippocampus using brain electrodes that according to its creators 'can boost performance on memory tests by up to 30 per cent' (Hamzelou, 2017). A 30 per cent enhancement to individual memory would affect PR practice. So would an exoskeleton improving movement and strength by 30 per cent. Or for that matter sensor patches, skins, gloves, implants or liquid-state devices that create 30 per cent better sensations of touch in prosthetic limbs (*inter alia* Kenry, Yeo & Lim, 2016; Burton, 2018). Whatever commercially viable forms such devices might take, PR will need to learn about them, and play with them. Are they media devices, message-carriers, perception shapers, target audiences or all four and more besides?

At least three areas of prosthetics could present opportunities for PR and hybridized individuals: the development of exoskeletons used by humans to accomplish particular tasks; neural implants that process larger volumes of information and supplement memory; prosthetics that stimulate human senses, including touch, hearing and sight. Disabled individuals may be among the first to benefit, but it is understood, not least by the military, that the new prosthetics 'could conceivably be used to enhance the memory, learning ability, concentration, and visual and auditory capabilities of able-bodied individuals' (Chase, 2007).

The value of this to PR is that increased use of prosthetics may be another way to overcome the 'uncanny valley' obstacle to societal acceptance described in Chapter 8. Prosthetics have a direct connection to the human mind that might help hybrid individuality cross the valley separating it from traditional, familiar and 'safe' forms of individuality. To be competitive, PR practitioners must recognize hybrid individuals as powerful or potential consumers, campaigners, voters and in other existing or yet-to-be-determined roles. Unwitting or deliberate, PR will be a force for accepting hybridized individuals with technologically enhanced mental and physical powers, and will itself change with the coming of hybridized individuality using implants, patches or exoskeletons, almost but not quite out of human recognition. Being wholly 'out of human recognition' might involve another step in PR's long effort to understand individuality.

Engaging with artificial consciousness

This book has described making machines conscious of their individuality, and fully independent of the human mind, and what it may mean for PR if further progress is made. It believes PR must reflect on the immense global effort now underway to build such machines. The builders are in government, the military, universities, corporations and PR must learn from the theoretical and mechanical work that has been done.

Is it ironic that the initial challenge of AI, and the one PR is perhaps best equipped to deal with, is uncertainty? In Stephen Hawking's words 'we cannot know if we will be infinitely helped by AI, or ignored by it and side-lined, or conceivably destroyed by it' (Hawking, 2017, 17:24). 'AI could develop a will of its own; a will that is in conflict with ours, and destroy us' (Hawking, 2017, 18:11). What part could any form of PR, let alone its influence over individuality, have in such an uncertain and automated world? Hawking proposed in 2017:

We need to employ best practice and effective management in all areas of its (AI's) development.

(Hawking, 2017, 3:15 18:45)

Is that enough? Can a social challenge be dealt with by engineering and management methods at the development stage? Should AI be left to scientists and regulatory agencies, any more than war should be left to generals? If the issue is too big for that, there must be tasks for PR. One is communication about acceptance. Conscious machines that do not look human and are not linked to the human brain are another route across the uncanny valley, to accepting their individuality because they are unlike humans and so less unsettling. This was the possibility Mori raised in his original paper. However, their activities might still trouble many people. Machines that, as one professor of electrical and computer engineering put it, 'replace humans at literally all jobs' (Kak, 2017) would certainly 'challenge the human-robot relationship' (Hawking, 2017, 21:31). They might conduct PR activities between themselves if they were seeking support from fellow machines in a competitive environment or managing issues of human concern that required machine empathy and cooperation, or deciding on a common attitude towards a human activity or possibly humans in general. Ceding such communication power would be as unsettling to human society as ceding control of military powers to machines, or when facing the less likely prospect of having no work to do. Exclusion from public discussion about subjects theoretically designed for our own good may be as large a long-term risk as outsourcing our ability to defend ourselves. The options are: to stop it from happening or to hope it does not happen; trying to preserve some level of supervision; to intervene in or and monitor all M2M PR to influence perceptions of artificially conscious agents when necessary, using human or machine communication activity in the public arena. PR would become one guarantor of a cooperative, public connection between two kinds of individuality who might otherwise exist in isolation or ignorance of each other's intentions and – in all probability – feelings. Exchanges of views or statements of positions that are accessible to society in general must be a prerequisite for a constructive connection between conscious AA and the conscious humanity they were originally meant to serve under or alongside, but not lead, unless powerful individuals change their minds.

It is not likely that all governments, institutions, companies or, say, campaigning nonprofits will encourage machine consciousness for exactly the same motives. Each organization has its own rules, jargon and political, military, commercial or social objectives. Machine individuality will reflect a wide range of motives. These should at least be publicly known. Fully communicated transparency is highly unlikely, but secrecy and artificial consciousness do not sit well together. As far as possible PR must be involved in one of its traditional roles of encouraging social harmony, this time by communicating with and between individually conscious machines of immense power. All forms of individuality must understand one another.

Using individuality to preserve a public sphere

Historically, PR offers organizations a useful economy of scale; a way to reach individuals by communicating through group identities that matter to them and through which they are most open to the subject being communicated. Media was designed to cultivate this profitable and increasingly necessary relationship between individual actions and group identity. Individuality took advantage of group political, social or economic benefits, and the ideas or employment that group contacts generated. As we have seen, the more complex the connections between individual and group, the more complex the communication of power and the more the individual needed to connect with group goals as consumer, employer and employee, silent citizen or social activist. This connection was bridged in part by PR methods that evolved into a distinct named profession with necessary specialties of its own to tackle complex tasks connecting individuals and groups.

No longer. The individual is learning to use media whose reach and creative potential was once the preserve of large organizations, and PR is looking for new ways to group people together on behalf of clients. The individual is better equipped to approach organisations on his or her own terms, forming connections that feel more real when they are more virtual. Physical isolation might matter less, physical location less still. *The Machine Stops* is a short story by E. M. Forster published in 1909. It is set in a future dominated by personal technology, and where the world's inhabitants find real people increasingly distasteful. 'The clumsy system of public gatherings had been long since abandoned' and people prefer to remain in separate rooms below ground that are 'filled with buttons and switches' for everything including communication. 'The room, though it contained nothing, was in touch with all that she cared for in the world' (Forster, 1909, I). This is an extreme, final, version of LeFevre's self-ownership mentioned in Chapter 4. It has become 'you who are ruled by yourself alone' in the words of the Rig Veda (Doniger, 1981, Varuna 7.86). It is an individual able to extend into communicating machines: an enormous expansion of selfhood. 'The man has a thousand heads, a thousand eyes, a thousand feet. He pervaded the earth on all sides and extended beyond it as far as ten fingers' (Doniger, 1981, Creation 10.90).

Dystopian for some, utopian for others, but communication with the external world is still needed. PR's basic approaches are the best means yet known to address the expansion of communication power by individuality: human or machine. This book has tried to point out some of the historical and future consequences of that expansion. The nub is that individuality itself continuously evolves, and must continuously be contacted in new ways by PR, whose own evolution is affected. At the moment many of the economies of scale offered by larger audiences are vanishing. Direct connections with individuality will be vital to maintain a public sphere for society as a whole.

Whether the individual is human or machine might not much matter. Alan Turing's famous test, described in his 1950 paper, is on course to reach the point where an interrogator in one room cannot tell from the answers if what is in the other room is machine or a human (Turing, 1950, pp. 433–434). From that moment, there must be public communication in society whether the questioner and answerers are a mix of human and machine, or all one or all another. PR, or a version of it blending data, persuasion, dialogue, often urgent and astonishing speed, and transparency, will be used to try and reach constructive cooperation on social issues, governance and the provision of goods and other commercial services in whatever form they take.

Self-ownership in a world of machines and human interaction in every social sphere begs LeFevre's more awkward follow-up question: 'If a man owns himself, why can't he own another?' (LeFevre, 1966/2007, Chapter IV). More troubling still if the question is asked by AI. In 1921 one of the first robot workers depicted in literature, Radius, advances to the stage of declaring 'I do not want a master. I know everything', immediately followed by 'I want to be the master of others', and finally: 'I want to be the master of people' (Čapek & Novack, 2004, Act I).

PR becomes more necessary if that particular problem is considered, and who or what will own whom if Turing's game is taken a stage further. Humans may well someday be unable to tell if they are working with humans and machines (which to an extent is now happening with bots following social media users); but suitably advanced individual machines will know the difference, and more-over will communicate between themselves in ways humans cannot follow, when the Turing test is not being conducted. The 2017 Facebook experiment described earlier raises that possibility.

Mutual comprehension often involves empathy. AI can learn to appeal to human emotion at least as effectively as reason: a procedure PR well understands. PR must participate in public communication because empathetic relations between forms of individuality will be navigated. Today simple robot toys or human-looking robots are made to encourage empathy from humans by using design and programmed behaviour. Our emotional connection to robots is at least a century old (older if Talos the doomed bronze automaton in Greek myth or the forlorn creature in Mary Shelley's 1818 novel *Frankenstein* are counted as arti-ficial), and appears in the 1921 Czech play *R.U.R. (Rossum's Universal Robots)*, where the word robot (originally the name of a compulsory labour law in the Austro-Hungarian Empire) was first used for all AAs like Radius (Čapek et al., 2004), through films, theatre, literature and manufacturing down to empathetic robots responding to human feeling. Robots like Pepper, a humanoid launched in 2014 and billed as 'kindly, endearing and surprising', 'a genuine day-to-day com-panion', 'capable of recognising the principal human emotions and adapting his behaviour to the mood of his interlocutor' (Softbank). Empathy's privileges extend to toy robots like Softbank's Nao, or Cozmo an AI robot made by Carnegie Mellon graduates and $200 million in venture capital (Madrigal, 2017, p. 26). The makers describe him as: 'Big brain. Bigger personality'; a 'gifted little guy with a mind of his own. He's a real-life robot like you've only seen in movies, with a one-of-a-kind personality that evolves the more you hang out' (Anki, 2017).

It seems quite easy to make some humans empathize with robots once the uncanny valley is crossed. Why should it be otherwise? History and prehistory shows that humans have empathized with animals, landscapes, toys, effigies, colours, buildings, trees, ideas, smells, sounds and other objects. Empathy with material and immaterial items is a universal human (and maybe extra-human) characteristic; a rational or irrational stimulus to modest or epoch shaking effort, and a social output of the individual's inner experiences, including human reason. It must be accepted that even relatively crude AI robots could attract the same sympathy.

Could PR for humans learn how to arouse reciprocal empathy from conscious AAs? Agents individually superior to humans in productivity, machine learning speed, programmed intelligence, speed and strength?

Empathy's role in human-AI relations is therefore another reason for PR to continue its work, whatever PR itself will be called in future, and whatever its fate as a discrete profession. Individual humans may feel empathy for machines and other things. Individual machines may not, or they might mechanically mimic it, or express themselves with feeling but in unfamiliar ways. AI's might need to learn empathy, suggested a science and technology writer, 'to make sure it [the AI-human relationship] stays friendly and peaceful' (Perry, 2016). Public communication seems essential for the same reason; more so given emotion's more dangerous possibilities, recognized by Hawking and others.

The threats presented by conscious AA was foreseen from the moment of their imagining, in *R.U.R.*, Karel Čapek's play which ushered in robot literature and the descriptor 'robot' for its indefatigable biomechanically grown workers. An idealist creates organic not mechanical robots with feeling, but the gift of greater humanity leads to hatred and rebellion. The individual human, instead of the chance to 'perfect your own being' and 'be the master of creation', is destroyed instead (Čapek et al., 2004, Prologue). The problems *R.U.R.* raised are still part of a debate connecting humans, machines, new media technology and organizations. The debate will continue long after the initial question about how best to manage the new machines is answered, in part by the machines themselves.

For the moment, PR is comparatively invisible on these subjects, including (except for distribution and accompanying publicity) the open letter drafted at 'The Future of AI conference' in 2015. 'Research Priorities for Robust and Beneficial Artificial Intelligence' was co-signed by Stephen Hawking and other luminaries of science and technology, and accompanied by a longer research priorities document (Russell et al., 2015). The longer document emphasizes that AI is a societal subject beyond science and technology and must be publicly discussed to establish bases for human relations with powerful AI, and ensure that it represents human values in key areas including law, economic growth and security (Russell et al., 2015).

In terms of historical importance it is possible to think of this document as a very public and more hopeful equivalent of the private letter signed by Albert Einstein and sent to President Franklin D. Roosevelt in August 1939, warning about German atomic research. It shows that PR has work to do, first in promoting public discussion about what the longer open document carefully calls 'robustness research' which is not-quite-reassuringly justified in the same way that home insurance is 'justified by a nonnegligible probability of the home burning down' (Russell et al., 2015, p. 109).

The publicity for conscious or part-conscious machines as products or brands, will also ensure organizations use PR to communicate familiarity with more advanced AA than Pepper and Cozmo. The fact that they too will do this is another reason PR in the public sphere is a means for ensuring society retains its collective purposes and manages collective debates as AA evolves higher forms of individual consciousness.

Make-believe and making belief

The fate of human individuality at the dawn of machine individuality requires a future for PR. If AAs, however conscious, take over much human work and solve many human problems, humans otherwise without purpose need a means to imagine and agree shared goals, act on them, and communicate about them with AAs. Historically, cultures without common purposes or a will to address challenges have trouble existing, let alone reproducing, which is another prospect raised in *R.U.R.*, and maybe encouraged by continuing refinements in robotics and virtual reality. The disillusioned manager of Čapek's robot factory in *R.U.R.* had set himself lofty goals, in which humans are 'unrestricted, free and supreme':

> I wanted there to be nothing, nothing, nothing left of that damned mess of a social hierarchy! I abhorred degradation and suffering! I was fighting against poverty!
>
> (Čapek et al., 2004, Act II)

PR's more achievable purpose may in part be to cultivate shared beliefs out of an enhanced individual capacity for make-believe. More individuals than ever before will use PR's techniques; retaining the Shannon–Weaver model in creative appeals to reason, emotion and imagination. PR can play its customary part as motivated individuals set goals, and will be needed, as it always has been, before during and after those goals have been reached. Whether or not AI delivers on its biggest promises of ending economic uncertainty (and economics itself) by eliminating scarcity and creating a true Cockaigne, the land of perpetual plenty dreamed of by hungry mediaeval minds, 'unrestricted, free and supreme' human individuality might think it prudent to retain responsibility for managing artificial consciousness. Other people might disagree: individuation is the adventure of becoming something distinct from something else. In an era of plentiful resources and possibly few restraints some may want to discover how far the adventure of individuation can go – are artificially conscious devices also entitled to the mixed blessings of self-ownership? PR could be used by somebody or something to remind society about alternative possibilities.

Nor can we tell if new forms of individuality, hybrid or machine, will have the same emotional and imaginative powers that humans feel and express. The individual for instance feels part of time and space, and this feeling whether it is absolutely true or not has led great people to do and express great things. Even a wilfully emptied mind, denying or mocking all learning, is an attempt to come to terms with these great facts of perception. Aspiration is a task for a lifetime and it is unavoidable. In the sixth century BC Confucius told his followers that at 30 'I set my mind upon learning'. Nevertheless, he was not free of doubts until 40; his 'ear was attuned' at 60 and finally, at 70, 'I could follow my heart's desires without overstepping the bounds of propriety' (Slingerland, 2003, 2.4).

If history is a guide, many individuals will share this view and communicate their deeds and beliefs. The ancient desire to manage public communication could be as strong as ever. Everything is becoming media, everyone is media, devices and humans are converging on communication, and converging inside us, or inside what characterizes us – an endless, sleepless stream of impressions, images, feelings, words, sounds. If we do not precisely know it works inside of us, we are at least committed to share messages outside of us, in groups or individually.

Another possibility for PR is, as the media moves further inside human or machine bodies, that we – we, not whatever content we may want to communicate – will become the main message, and the sum of external experiences and contacts. We may build our own inner worlds, more meaningful than the world outside; we might willingly convert ourselves into a pure media platform for organizations, brands and other people. More and more of our inner life will be lived outside, open to others and up for sale, or for influence.

How should organizations build and fit into a more vivid world of 'public imagination' to guide individual choices? One answer is to make belief in organization, or their products, by using make-believe in older, almost forgotten ways. To penetrate human imagination in the way prehistoric humans penetrated caves and left messages there that even now mean something to us. Organizations must discover, and are discovering, how to use make-believe to encourage desire more personally or privately. This involves making signs and symbols more personal or private, since public platforms designed for groups may paradoxically not be needed for public communication. Conforming group behaviour to protect brand reputation for example will be harder for organizations to achieve. A realistic alternative is 'embracing individuality' in its own right, the liberating approach a *Sports Illustrated* commentator recommended to the US National Football League during the players' 2017 season anthem protests (Klemko, 2017, p. 23).

Future PR may evoke a spiritual dimension to encourage choice-making, in accordance with individuality's increased desire and power to conjure and transmit dreams, visions or fears using media and other intelligent devices about to join with our biology. Reason is not perfect. Society's future will not solely belong to engineers, scientists or AAs. Not if the uncertainties of wayward human individuality and its risks and rewards continue to be valued. 'The wise man looks in the cup of Reason', wrote the blind mediaeval freethinker and poet Abul ʿAla Al-Maʿarri (973–1057), who valued Reason above religion, 'but the one who looks to his brother will see truth, or perhaps lies' (Al-Ma'arri & Smith, 2015, p. 127).

Other questions remain open for PR. A communication risk of scientific reason is that applying neuroscience, cognitive science, AI and internet-brain technology erodes our sense of past and future and gratifies many individuals in a permanent present, isolated and sated by streams of sensations and soundbites. Or will versions of aspiration triumph? Will most of us guard our inner life and personal autonomy by being more reflective, wiser, moderate and measured and by sharing our ideas? Will something ineradicable in our inner life still prompt us to seek out groups, if only groups relying on capricious and fleeting individual attachments? What precisely will PR do with such aspirations if group-directed media platforms fall into disuse? The questions cannot be answered in detail, not until the question asked in Chapter 1 is answered by events: will any of the coming changes to individuality encourage open and incredibly creative kinds of PR? One way or another, aspects of our individuality shaped by PR's past and present push uncomfortably against a future which may be hard for PR to accept but which at the moment looks more likely to come than not. Pretending this is not happening is unhelpful.

References

Al-Maʿarri, A. A., & Smith, P. (2015). *The book of al-Maʿarri.* Campbell Creek, Victoria: New Humanity Books.

Alchian, A. (1950). Uncertainty, evolution, and economic theory. *Journal of Political Economy, 58*(3), 211–221. Retrieved from www.jstor.org/stable/1827159.

Anki. (2017). Meet Cozmo. Retrieved from www.anki.com/en-ca/cozmo.

Bernays, E. L. (2005). *Propaganda.* Kindle Book. New York: Ig Publishing.

Burton, B. (2018, 4 January). Bionic hand with sense of touch can be worn outside the lab. *CNET.* Retrieved from www.cnet.com/news/bionic-hand-sense-touch-worn-outside-lab-prosthetics/.

Čapek, K., & Novack, C. (2004). *R.U.R. (Rossum's universal robots).* London: Penguin Books.

Carandini, M. (2012). From circuits to behavior: A bridge too far? *Nature Neuroscience, 15*(4), 507–509. doi:10.1038/nn.3043.

Chase, V. D. (2007, 13 February). The ethics of neural prosthetics. The Hastings Center. Retrieved from www.thehastingscenter.org/the-ethics-of-neural-prosthetics/?s=.

Doniger, W. (1981). *The Rig Veda: an anthology.* eBook. London: Penguin.

Forster, E. M. (2016). *The machine stops.* eBook. London: Jovian Press.

Hamzelou, J. (2017, 13 November). Brain implant boosts human memory by mimicking how we learn. *New Scientist.* Retrieved from www.newscientist.com/article/2153034-brain-implant-boosts-human-memory-by-mimicking-how-we-learn/.

Hawking, S. (2017, 6 November). 'Web Summit 2017. Inaugural opening conference'. Websummit. Lisbon, Portugal. Retrieved from: www.youtube.com/watch?v=FSI42 Kw22Pw.

Henson, R. (2005). What can functional neuroimaging tell the experimental psychologist? *Quarterly Journal of Experimental Psychology*, *58*A, 193–233. Retrieved from https://pdfs.semanticscholar.org/d5f0/9180c9618882c9ce813856093289c83bbd84.pdf.

Kak, S. (2017, 15 December). Will artificial intelligence become conscious? *Singularity-Hub*. Retrieved from https://singularityhub.com/2017/12/15/will-artificial-intelligence-become-conscious/#sm.014vmf7o16ylcus104016qn7femw5.

Kenry, Yeo, J. C., & Lim, C. T. (2016). Emerging flexible and wearable physical sensing platforms for healthcare and biomedical applications. *Microsystems & Nanoengineering*, *2*, 16043. doi:http://dx.doi.org.ezp.bentley.edu/10.1038/micronano. 2016.43.

Keynes, J. (2016). The end of laissez-faire. In Keynes, J. *Essays in Persuasion*. eBook. London: Palgrave Macmillan UK.

Klemko, R. (2017). The Case for … EMBRACING INDIVIDUALITY. *Sports Illustrated*, *127*(13), 23.

Knight, F. H. (1921). *Risk, uncertainty and profit*. eBook. Chicago: Hart, Schaffner & Marx.

Kovaka, K. (2015). Biological individuality and scientific practice. *Philosophy of Science*, *82*(5), 1092–1103.

Krakauer, J. W., Ghazanfar, A. A., Gomez-Marin, A., MacIver, M. A., & Poeppel, D. (2017). Neuroscience needs behavior: Correcting a reductionist bias. *Neuron*, *93*(3), 480–490. doi:10.1016/j.neuron.2016.12.041.

LeFevre, R. (1966/2007). *The philosophy of ownership*. eBook. Auburn, AL: Ludwig von Mises Institute.

Madrigal, A. C. (2017, December). My son's first robot. For better and worse, toys power by AI are building emotional bonds with children. *The Atlantic*, 26–27.

Marr, D. (1982). *Vision: A computational approach*. New York: Freeman.

Marx, K., Engels, F., & Hobsbawm, E. J. (1998). *The Communist manifesto: A modern edition*. London: Verso.

von Mises, L. (1949/1966). *Human action: A treatise on economics*. Third Edition. Chicago: Regnery.

Ormerod, P. (2015). The economics of radical uncertainty. *Economics: The Open-Access, Open-Assessment E-Journal*, 91–20.

Perry, P. (2016). Can AI develop empathy? *Bigthink.com*. Retrieved from http://bigthink.com/philip-perry/can-ai-develop-empathy.

Russell, S. (2015, 12 January). An open letter. Research Priorities for robust and beneficial artificial intelligence. Retrieved from https://futureoflife.org/ai-open-letter.

Russell, S., Dewey, D., & Tegmark, M. (2015). Research Priorities for Robust and Beneficial Artificial Intelligence. *AI Magazine*, *36*(4), 105–114. Retrieved from https://futureoflife.org/data/documents/research_priorities.pdf?x57718.

Slingerland, E. (2003). *Confucius analects*. Indianapolis. IN: Hackett Publishing.

Softbank Robotics. (2017). Who is Pepper? Retrieved from www.ald.softbankrobotics.com/en/robots/pepper.

Turing, A. (1950). Computing machinery and intelligence. *Mind*, *59*(236), 433–460. Retrieved from www.jstor.org/stable/2251299.

Weisberg, D. S., Keil, F. C., Goodstein, J., Rawson, E., & Gray, J. R. (2008). The seductive allure of neuroscience explanations. *Journal of Cognitive Neuroscience*, *20*(3), 470–477. http://doi.org/10.1162/jocn.2008.20040.

Index

cognition 14, 29, 46, 63, 69, 70, 71, 95–96;
  see also mental processes
cognitive enhancement 94, 125–126
cognitive science 69, 70–71, 72, 116; and
  PR 68–72
collaboration 13, 30, 88, 95, 101, 111
collective recall 31
color perception 38
communication (s): and artificial agents
  (AA) 112–113; and artificial intelligence
  (AI) 5, 116; by artificial intelligences
  127; changing possibilities for 104; and
  choice 80; of conformity 46–49; and
  consciousness 12–16, 14; creative
  approaches to 112–113; of dominance
  54; and the emotions 36; evolution of 5;
  group 11, 30; hierarchical levels of 117;
  and individuality 99; and inner speech
  63; instincts for 15; of knowledge 11;
  and language 68; managed 27–28,
  42–43, 50, 55; Mathematical theory of
  61; organized 23; and power 43; of
  power 45, 53, 128; and PR 122; PR as
  97–98; public 9, 12, 20, 28, 42–43, 50,
  55, 97, 116, 132; public/group 3–4;
  quantitative 36; revolution in 10;
  strategic 49
competition 13–15
complexity: connections with 60–62; as
  dynamic process 60; in emotion 59;
  evolution of 61; fragility of 60–61;
  individual 60, 62; inside organizations
  62; of the mind 59–60; in reasoning 59,
  62–64; social 62
compulsion 81–82
conformity: benefits of 44, 48–49; and
  choice 79–80; communication of 46–49;
  neurological rewards of 46
Confucius 45, 46–49, 132
consciousness: and communication 12–16,
  14; creative 11; defined 6; dynamic 13;
  fragmenting 15; hard problem of 67; in
  humanlike machines 113; indeterminate
  66, 111; individual 1, 23–24, 27–28, 65;
  of individuality 12; mind-brain 66; and
  PR 16– 19
conscious satisfaction or suffering (CSS)
  113
consent engineers 105, 109
consumerism 44
conversion through symbolization 18–19
creativity 37, 69, 71, 89, 99, 102, 105, 115,
  119
culture: collective 96; group 96; human 20;

and individuality 102–103; material 17,
  96; oral vs. literate 31; organizational
  19; power and 50, 54; and PR 2, 18;
  Statist 102; values of 16; westernized
  101
Cutler, Howard 16
cybernetics 115

dark energy 29
Darwin, Charles 77
data mining 104–105
data visualization 69
Datini, Francesco di Marco 100
decision making: and brain physiology
  87; and emotions 80; episodic 87; and
  the Information Revolution 84;
  memory-based 87; shared 118; value-
  based 87
Default Mode Network (DMN) 34
Delacour, Jean 23–24
de Maistre, Joseph 17
Descartes, René 12, 13
determinism 64, 66
dialogue 14, 75, 82, 83, 89–90, 104, 111,
  113, 114, 117, 119, 122, 129; internal
  63; machine 70
diversity 61, 95, 115, 116
dominance 17, 42, 54; emotional 52–53;
  see also power
dopamine 17
dream analysis 15
drugs, cognitive-enhancing 71
Dynamic Causal Modeling (DCM) 88

Edelman, Richard 84
Einstein, Albert 130
emotion (s): and communication 26;
  complexity in 59; as contagion 36–39;
  and decision making 80; languages of
  37–38; and meaning-making 67; moral
  52; negative 80–81; perception of
  37–38; and PR 33–35; and reason 35;
  regulation of 80; as 'truth' 35–36
emotional climate 80
emotional contagion 34, 36–39, 38
emotional dominance 52–53; *see also*
  dominance
empathy 34, 127, 129–130
empowerment 44; *see also* power
Engels, Friedrich 9, 62, 123
engineering 116; and artificial agents (AA)
  119–120; of consent 105
enhancement: of cognition 94; of
  individuality 98, 100; of the individual